"When they shoot us, will it hurt?"

Raya Rolnikaite, age 10, to her mother
on their way to Ponary, Lithuania, extermination camp
September 23, 1943

MARIA ROLNIKAITE (MASHA ROLNIK)

ABOUT 1946   ABOUT 1960

ABOUT 1985

I Must Tell

(Reconstituted Diary 1941-1945)

MARIA ROLNIKAITE
(MASHA ROLNIK)

A Documentary Narrative

Translated from the Russian,
with Biography and Introduction, by:

DANIEL H. SHUBIN

Maria Rolnikaite

Cover photo 1940

ISBN 978-1-387-69337-5
Copyright 2018
Daniel H. Shubin

Email: danhshubin at yahoo dot com

TABLE OF CONTENTS

1. INTRODUCTION BY THE TRANSLATOR   9

2. BIOGRAPHY OF MARIA ROLNIKAITE   13

3. INTRODUCTION BY ILYA EHRENBURG   17

4. *I MUST TELL*   23

5. *INTERVIEW WITH MARIA ROLNIKAITE*   237

ROLNIKAITE FAMILY PHOTO; CIRCA 1938

Sitting:
Grandfather Abel and grandmother Hannah Rolnikaite;

Standing:
Mother Taiba Aaronovna, Uncle Mikhel Rolnikaite, older sister Miriam, related boy, Uncle Berel Rolnikaite, Uncle Meyer Rolnikaite, Maria (Masha) Rolnikaite, father Grigori Rolnikaite.

The Parents of Maria Rolnikaite:

Grish (Grigori) Abelovich and Taiba Aaronovna Rolnikas

Grigori Rolnikaite as a soldier in the Red Army after the Germans invaded Lithuania.

Maria Rolnikaite (Masha Rolnik) was born in Klaipeda, Lithuania. She lived in Vilnius most of her life, and in the ghetto during the German occupation. She was then moved to NAZI concentration camps Kaiserwald and Strasdenhof in the Riga, Latvia, area. After evacuation she was taken to the Baltic Sea coast where she and other inmates were taken by ship to NAZI extermination camp Stutthof, near Gdansk, Poland. With the movement of Soviet Red Army troops, she was moved west, until liberated in Lanz, Germany.

INTRODUCTION

(BY THE TRANSLATOR)

After returning from concentration camps, and after Soviet authorities investigated her and assigned her new documents, Maria Rolnikaite (Masha Rolnik) copied all of her surviving notes, letter by letter, into three large notebooks and hid them in a box. Maria was able to recover her notebooks that she left with Mr Jonaitus in Vilnius, and some other scattered fragments from the old apartment in Vilnius and the one in the ghetto. But anything else compiled after her relocation to Riga camps after the liquidation of the Vilnius ghetto was lost.

It was not until 15 years after her release from Stutthof extermination camp and her return home that she started with the reconstruction of the complete diary. Maria reconstructed her entire diary based on the surviving notebooks and her memory. The reconstructed diary now developed into something more that its original intent. It evolved into a stream-of-consciousness documentary narrative, of the experiences, thoughts, fears and feelings of a Lithuanian Jewish girl, beginning a month before her 14th birthday, and for the next 3 years, 7 months, and 15 days.

The diary is beyond the normal scope of literature because Maria wrote as she felt at the time in that particular environment, as well as regarding the events occurring around her, whether having a direct or indirect impact on her situation. No doubt it was extremely difficult for Maria to accomplish this by having to relive all the events on an individual basis and then record it as if it was occurring right then and there, putting her feelings of the moment on paper.

When Maria was rescued from Nazi occupation as an inmate, she was 17 years and 6 months of age, unable to walk due to her swollen legs, barely able to speak, her front teeth were knocked out, she was dehydrated and malnourished. Maria's torso was a skeleton covered with emaciated skin. The pain of the years under the brutal treatment of the Nazi regime left her both physically and emotionally devastated, her healing and recovery took a while until she was well enough to return into society and enter school again and start a career.

Her diary was first published until the title of, *Vilna Diary, 1941-1945*, in the Lithuanian language in 1963. Maria then translated it into both Yiddish and Russian herself. The initial Russian publication under the title *I Must Tell* was in the magazine *Zvesda* (Star) in 1965, this was 20 years after the end of the war. Subsequently the book was translated into an additional 15 languages.[1] The initial version of *I Must Tell* was edited by Soviet censurers, and a complete unedited version was finally published in Russian in 2013.[2]

This is the saddest book you will ever read.

Of all the 20 books that I have translated from Russian into English or written on Russian biography, religion and philosophy, this is the saddest. If you the reader do not have tears streaming down your cheeks at least a dozen times by the time you read the final line, you are lacking immensely in pathos, or you just do not contain human emotion. You have to be callous to human suffering. If it is not heart-wrenching, or causing you to become nauseous on occasion at the descriptions of human suffering and misery, at the unbelievable brutality and ruthlessness of what one human is doing and imposing on another, it is time to face reality. This book is reality.

---

[1] This volume is the first translation into English.
[2] This translator used the Russian 2016 version, published by *Samokat*, Moscow, the edition authorized in 2015 by Maria Rolnikaite prior to her death.

This is the first translation into English, over 60 years since its original publication. I have the impression this is because the American public would prefer the sanitized version of a diary such as Anna Frank's, who hid in an attic, rather than face the brutal reality and atrocities of Maria Rolnikaite's world. She watched people be erased from existence and history, and for no cause, no reason, no purpose, just because someone having a greater authority wanted them out of existence. She watched herself face the same type of deprivation of life's benefits on a regular basis, and faced being selected for execution on several occasions and the decision was often arbitrary.

Maria Rolnikaite survived the final occasions of her possible death because a Nazi officer told the soldier not to shoot her since the sound of the gunshot to her head might alert the Red Army to their location. So the soldier just kicked Maria into a ditch to freeze overnight, but then another woman in the same predicament exerted the effort to pull her out. So she survived the final attempt of the Nazis to erase her from existence. And maybe this occurred this way because divine providence wanted her to remain to relate her story to the rest of the world, as so she titled her the publication of her diary – *I Must Tell*. Maybe her survival of 3 years and 7-1/2 months under German occupation, and in concentration and extermination camps, and travel between them, and what occurred to her own family, was divine providence for her to relate the extremity of human unconscionable brutality possible. Without her exposure to all of this, it may also have become forgotten, and become of non-existent. As if it never occurred.

The innocence and naivety of a teenage girl is also noticeable in the text, how quite often Maria accepts something at face value, but then the deception behind it surfaces. On a regular basis she will disclose German schemes and efforts as another deception.

Maria Rolnikaite also resurrects the death. She bring back to life those that perished at the hands of the Nazis solely because of their nationality or some arbitrary reason, by telling us about them. Not to be forgotten.

Maybe my own effort for this work was also a piece of divine providence. I never heard of Maria Rolnikaite, not my whole life, until I read a biography of Ilya Ehrenburg who mentioned her and her diary. Then something inside of me said to further investigate her and I discovered that no English translation was accomplished to date. Something inside of me said the same – I must tell.

This translation is different because it is a different type of book. A diary is not composed for others to read, like a novel or even an autobiography. It is created for personal reasons, for recording personal issues and likes and dislikes and reactions and feelings and surmises and fears and consolations. I have used the language that a 14 to 17 year-old teenager would use, the style a girl would use to compose a dairy, the manner she reflects her thoughts, her stream of consciousness. If reading it is clumsy, it is because this is how her diary relates the information, how she provides her feelings to the reader.
  The only additions to the text are in [brackets] as necessary for the reader to better understand the content.

As a supplement to the diary, I have included an English translation of Ilya Ehrenburg's *Introduction* to the Russian version, and also an *Interview* done with Maria by Tatyana Voltskaya in 2003, both of which are very valuable and informative.

DANIEL H. SHUBIN
April 18, 2018

BIOGRAPHY OF MARIA ROLNIKAITE

(MASHA ROLNIK)

(BY THE TRANSLATOR)

Maria Grigoryevna Rolnikaite (Masha Grishko Rolnik in Yiddish) was born in Klaipeda, Lithuania, July 21, 1927.

Her father was Grish Abelovich Rolnikas, an attorney, and known as Grigori (1898-1973), and her mother was Taiba Aaronovna (1897-1943). Grigori and Taiba had 5 children: daughter Miriam (1924-2012), daughter Maria, called Masha in the diary (1927-2016), daughter Raya, called Rayechka in the diary (1933-1943), son Ruvim, called Ruvik in the diary (1935-1943), and one other son Aaron who died shortly after childbirth.

She attended school in Plunge before moving to Vilnius.

Her father moved to Vilnius to expand his attorney practice, and was a high profile figure in defending many people who were considered having questionable political views, but whom Grigori Rolnikaite felt had civil rights and a good defense. With the occupation of Vilnius by German military on June 24, 1941, Rolnikaite was separated from his family. Unable to return to

Vilnius due to the occupation, he joined the Soviet Red Army and fought against the Germans. He never saw his wife or son Ruvik or daughter Raya after that date. Eventually he remarried after the end of the war and rejoined with both his daughters Miriam and Maria.

Following the events of the diary, the remaining members of the Rolnikaite family: mother Taiba, daughters Miriam, Raya (Rayechka), Maria (Masha) and son Ruvim (Ruvik), kept together in the Vilnius ghetto. Sometime the middle of September 1943, Miriam succeeded in escaping the ghetto. With the liquidation of the Vilnius ghetto on September 23, Maria was separated from her mother and younger siblings, and was taken to concentration camps near Riga, Latvia: Kaiserwald initially and then Strasdenhof.

Mother Taiba, along with daughter Raya and son Ruvik, were executed at Ponary, Lithuania, extermination camp, in late September 1943.

With the evacuation of the Strasdenhof camp on August 5, 1944, Maria was taken by ship to Stutthof extermination camp, near Gdansk (Danzig), Poland. While there during the summer and autumn of 1944 she worked at a local estate doing farm labor. She returned to the camp in November and remained there until the approach of the Red Army in mid-January 1945. She was evacuated from Stutthof on January 25, and started walking west with the balance of the inmates, until liberated on March 10, 1945, at Lanz, Germany. She walked a distance of about 300 miles in 45 days.

Marie was 3 years and 7-1/7 months total under Nazi occupation and prison.

Maria returned to Vilnius later that month, riding on the top of a railway box car. Once arriving she was interviewed by the Soviet secret police for her activities in Germany. She survived without formal identification and a passport until finally cleared of all possible charges by the Soviet government.

She received total clearance on May 20, 1945. She also rejoined her father and his new wife and sister Miriam. She completed her elementary education attending night school while working during the day.

In 1955, in Vilnius, Maria completed the Gorki Literary Institute and spent the next decade living there. She worked as an editor and director of art for the Ministry of Culture of Lithuania and with publications of books (1945-48), then later assisting the Vilnius Philharmonic (1948-64). She also translated Soviet authors into both Lithuanian and Yiddish.

Maria moved to Leningrad in 1964, and lived there until her death in 2016. She was the sole writer, collector and distributor of literature dealing with the holocaust and heroism of the Jewish community during that period. She was also active in the anti-fascist movement and the Jewish community of Leningrad.

Maria eventually married and after she moved to Leningrad. Her husband was Semeon Savelyevich Tzukernik. He was born in Leningrad in 1922, and served in the Soviet military assigned to the Far East and retired having the rank of First Lieutenant. He then attended Polytechnical Institute and became an engineer. He passed away in 2008.

After a short illness, Maria Rolnikaite died of natural causes on April 7, 2016; she was 88 years of age. She is buried at the Preobrazhenski Jewish Cemetery in St Petersburg, alongside her husband.

Maria gave several presentations in Germany, Lithuania, Latvia and France on her experiences during World War 2. She also gave seminars on the evils of anti-Semitism and promoted toleration between religions and nationalities. After *I Must Tell*, Maria wrote and published 6 more books, semi-fictional, based on her experiences before and after the years of World War 2:

Three Encounters, 1970
Adjusting to the Light, 1974
Long Silence, 1981
Matrimonial Protocol, 1990
This is all True, 2002
Alone with My Memory, 2013

Maria Rolnikaite, about 2014, at age 86.

INTRODUCTION BY ILYA EHRENBURG

(Translated from the Russian)

In France, Poland, Czechoslovakia, and in other countries, many fictional compositions were published, dozens of movies filmed, all showing the massive annihilation of the Jews by Nazis. Among them are several that are successful, but the writer or film artist is not given the ability to reincarnate the event: art has its laws and it stops in its creative representations with those scenes that lie beyond the limits of humanity's comprehension.

As I wrote in my book of recollections along with the late Vasili Semeonovich Grossman, we started during the war years to gather documents that described the annihilation of the Jewish population executed by the Nazis on Soviet territory occupied by the German army. These were letters written before they died, the narratives of a few that survived, diaries, Riga artists, Kharkov students, old men, girls. We titled the collection *The Black Book*. With the closure of the Jewish Anti-Fascist Committee, the collected, paginated and partially printed book was destroyed. Fortunately, I was able to preserve many of the original documents. Now *The Black Book* is being prepared for its publication. I feel that it will stir the consciences of those readers who have already started to forget the terrifying years of fascism. There is nothing artificial about the book, nothing invented: it is the result of a pile of papers upon which the truth of the events were written.

Masha Rolnikaike's diary was published in Vilnius in the Lithuanian language, and at the beginning of the year 1965, the Leningrad magazine *Zvezda* (Star) published it in Russian. These are not the author's fantasies, as incredible as they may read, but the truthfulness of the description of life in the ghetto and all that the 14-year old girl lived through. These experiences forced her to meditate, observe and be silent about her early years.

The diary of Anna Frank was also written by a girl and it was released to the public early. But in her diary there is no description of ghetto life, no mass murders, no death camps. This captive girl played at love, at life, even reading literature, while behind the walls an ominous search for hidden Jews was being pursued. Anna Frank's *Diary* was preserved by a Dutch woman and it was published just as it is, so that human memory or some editor's involvement would not affect the text. The diary of this girl with her innocent truthfulness shook the minds of millions of readers.

The well-meaning and courageous Jonaitis,[3] one of Masha's teachers, preserved the first notebook composing the diary, which described the initial horrible years. Then Masha, on her mother's advice, started to memorize what she wrote, but she did not have every opportunity to write and did not always remember everything word for word. Her diary she restored and compiled after her liberation, and at this time she was 18 years of age. Of course, she was not able to precisely recollect all of her feelings as a 15-year old girl by this time. However her diary is exceptionally valuable due to the details of the course of the life of tens of thousands of persons in the ghetto. Some submissively awaited death; others hoped for a miracle; a

---

[3] Henrikas Jonaitis, 1913-1993. In 1980 he as designated a Righteous Man among the Nations by the state of Israel.

third group fought back, as did Wittenberg, one of the heroes of the Resistance.[4]

Masha was the daughter of a progressive Vilnius attorney who more than once defended communists in court. Even though her personal and family name in Yiddish is Masha Rolnik, it was extended and modified to Maria Rolnikaite in the Russian and Lithuanian editions.

While still in school Masha was enthused with literature, and then later she finished the Literary Institute. But what the title indicates is that Masha almost always barricaded her diary from literary inserts. This is obvious when reading the content.

After the German occupation of many cities and regions of Ukraine and Russia the Germans under Hitler's order gathered Jews and executed them by shooting. This occurred in Kiev, Kharkov, Dnepropetrovsk, Gomel, and Smolensk and other cities. In Riga, Vilnius, Siauliai,[5] Kaunas,[6] and Minsk, the Germans built ghettos, placed Jews in workhouses, and gradually killed them. The masses that were executed by shooting were labeled as – *actionaries*.

Before the [Russian] Revolution Vilnius was a Russian provincial city and was the capital of Lithuania for a short while. The Poles captured the city at the end of the year 1920; while in 1939, it was again incorporated into Lithuania.

From ancient times Vilnius was counted among the most mature of centers of Jewish culture. The Nazi Rosenberg found there a large quantity of ancient books and valuable manuscripts. There is no precise statistics of the number of Jews the Nazis killed. Only a few survived. The city was occupied by German forces in the initial days of the war.

---

[4] Yitzhak Wittenburg, 1907 · July 16, 1943. He was a Jewish resistance fighter in Vilnius at this time.

[5] Or Shavli or Sauli. The fourth largest city in Lithuania, located in the north central part of the country.

[6] The second largest city in Lithuania, located in the geographical center of the country.

Vilnius was liberated in July 1944, after a sixty-day hand to hand combat struggle. At the time I encountered a regiment of Jewish partisans in the city. They told me that about 500 young men and women fled from the ghetto and joined the ranks of the partisans. The entire balance of the ghetto captives – about 80,000 – were killed by the Nazis in Ponary,[7] not far from Vilnius.[8]

In describing how she was forced to leave her mother, Masha wrote, "I weep. What did I do? What did mama do? Or other people? Is it really possible to kill someone just because of their nationality? Where did this barbaric hate toward us evolve? Why?" So did the 16-year old girl ask and this is not a futile question. Twenty years passed from the day of the demolition of Hitler's empire that again and now in Western Germany and in other countries of the world a web of swastikas are appearing over the memorials of the tortured, and old conversations have resurrected saying that the Jews are the reason for all of [Germany's] misfortunes.[9]

May Masha's book, one of many documents showing the years that obscured rationale and conscious, this contempt toward all of humanity, remind us of what the Polish poet Tuwin said, "Anti-Semitism is the international language of fascism."[10] Let it remind us that until every ghost of racism and fascism disappears, not one mother – whether Jewish or Arian or black or white – will be able to calmly look at her children. During her final minutes Masha's younger sister Rayechka asked her mother, "When they shoot us, will it hurt?"

May these words never be repeated.

ILYA EHRENBURG

---

[7] Presently known as Paneriai, a village presently in the Smorgonski region, Grognenski Province, Belarus.

[8] In addition to the Jews there were about 20 thousand Poles and 8 thousand Russian POWs executed by the Nazis.

[9] This would be the year 1965.

[10] Julian Tuwim, 1894-1953, a Polish poet of Jewish descent.

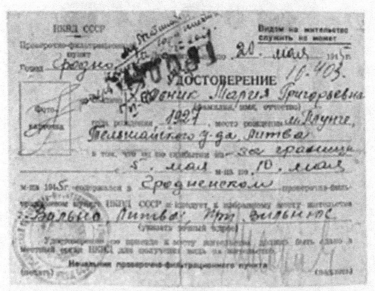

Справка проверочно-фильтрационного пункта НКВД от 20 мая 1945 года

Clearance from the National Commissariat of Internal Affairs, dated May 20, 1945, returning Maria Rolnikaite to normal affairs in the Soviet Union after her return from Germany.

The type of badge worn by Maria Rolnikaite
during the Vilnius ghetto.

I Must Tell

TO THE MEMORY OF MY MOTHER, SISTER AND BROTHER

MARIA ROLNIKAITE
(MASHA ROLNIK)

(Translated from the Russian)

First Page of the Diary of Maria Rolnikaite published in Russian, in the Magazine *Zvesda* (Star), 1965, Volume 2.

It was early morning, June 22, 1941. The sun shined joyously. No doubt from pride as it awakened the entire city and brought it into motion. I stand at the gates of our home. Like a sentry. Of course I am not alone, but with a neighbor from Apartment Number 8. Recently everybody has been on guard. Even us, schoolchildren. With the blare of an air raid alarm the sentries are responsible to summon passers-by and have them enter the yards to vacate the street.

I thought that standing guard would be interesting, but in reality it was very boring. The neighbor obviously did not consider me to be a suitable conversationalist and was reading a magazine. I did not bring a book as I had my fill of reading while studying for examinations.

I stare at the passers-by. I try to guess where they are hurrying, what they are thinking. And all the while I glance at my watch, that as soon as my guard duty ends I am running to the Nieola. We previously agreed to go swimming there.[11]

Suddenly the siren blared. A second, a third, each with its own voice, and it was so strange, so unpleasant. I watch, the neighbor walks into the street. I ran also. I am summoning everyone into the yard, but almost no one hears me. But it is not bad, at least they are not delaying but hurrying forward somewhere. Finally the street is desolate.

I stand in the yard and wait for the all-clear signal. I stare at all of my guests, overhearing their conversations. My God. They are talking about the war! It is apparent the alarm was not just a rehearsal, but the real thing! They already bombed Kaunas.[12]

I rush upstairs, to my home. Everyone already knows...

---

[11] Probably the Neris River which flows through Vilnius.
[12] June 22, 1941

The war... How am I supposed to live during a war? Will I still be able to attend school?

The alarm continued for a long time. The all-clear signal could not come soon enough.

Again the sirens started to blare. Several deafening hits were heard. Papa says that they are now bombing the city, but the bombs seems to be falling at some distance from us. However for us to just sit at home is dangerous, especially on the third floor. We need to go outside.

Almost all the residents of our tenement building were gathered outside. Even some with suitcases and bundles. Where are they going on a day like this? Mama explains that they are not going anywhere. They just took some of their most essential items, so if the building is bombed, they will not remain with nothing at all. But why did we not take anything?

I notice enemy airplanes.

I am terrified: I am afraid of the bombs. Having heard the whistle of an approaching bomb, I stop breathing. It seems it was going to fall right on our roof. The deafening sound of a hit and I again start to fear the next bomb.

Finally the airplanes fly away. We walk upstairs to our apartment to have breakfast. I eat and am hardly able to hold my tears. Perhaps this will be our final breakfast. Even if they don't kill us in the process, there will still be nothing to eat. All the grocery stores are closed.

Again the air raid alarm blares. We go downstairs to the yard. But they did not bomb this time. What a long day!

Just before evening the fascist airplanes became even more brazen. They did not turn any attention to our antiaircraft weapons and flew at low altitude over the city and bombed it. Nevertheless once I had the nerve to stick my head into the street and look into the sky. The airplanes were flying by, scattering what appeared to be a handful of walnuts, they were small bombs.

Suddenly pounding so loud that even the glass shook. Our neighbor, an engineer, said that the bomb fell nearby, probably on Bolshoi St.

It started to get dark, now it was night, but no one was getting ready to go home to sleep.

On occasion the darkness was scattered by the crisscross of searchlights. They would slither across the sky as if searching for something. Some would move slowly and with some precision, others would just plainly flicker or quickly move left to right and then right to left. Papa says they are looking for enemy planes. I tightly clench my eyes and not look at the sky. Only then do I not feel that war is occurring. It was warm as a regular summer night. But normally I would be long asleep by this time.

The soft hum of the airplanes. The prolonged and penetrating whistle. It is getting closer, closer, suddenly a flash of light illuminates the area and... A boom! Again a whistle! A boom! Whistle! Boom! One more! The antiaircraft guns retaliate, the bombs whistle, glass is falling from the windows. The noise is infernal.

Finally it is quiet, the airplanes have flown away.

The dawn brings light. The war rages on but the sun still rises. Everyone decided that where we are is not a safe enough place, it would be better to go into the building on the other side of the street where they have a basement.

One person at a time needs to run across the street. I say farewell to mama as she will run with Rayechka,[13] while papa with Ruvik. Miriam and I are older and we will run on our own. Shivering we hurry.

In reality it was not so scary in the basement. The whistles and the booms were not heard. But it was dirty, dusty and asphyxiating there. Those sitting closer to the doors would often go upstairs and take a look at what was happening.

---

[13] Her proper name Raya means paradise in Russian, Rayechka means little paradise

Finally they announced that all was quiet. The adults exited first and would run home and bring food to their families. There was just no way for any of us to survive any further without some breakfast.

Mama and papa also went home.

Mama was in tears when she returned. She said that we could now leave from there, it seems that no more bombing would happen. The Soviet army was retreating, the city will soon be occupied by German troops. This was a great misfortune, because they are cruel animals and viciously hate Jews. Other than this papa was actively involved with the Soviet government. He was an attorney. Even during the Smetonov era government[14] he was more than once threatened with retaliation because he defended in court underground communists because they were members of the MOPR.[15]

Now what will the occupiers do to him?

Mama accompanies us home. She calms down, she says that the fascists cannot do anything to him, because we are leaving into the center of the country and where they cannot reach us. Papa is leaving to join the resistance, and when the war ends, all of us will return home.

Mama is gathering a small bundle of clothing for each of us and tying to it our winter coats. We are waiting for papa. He went to buy us tickets.

Along the street Soviet tanks, automobiles and weapons are rushing in the direction of the Holy Gates. Already several hours have passed, but papa has not returned. It is obvious that it is difficult to get tickets: everyone wants to leave. But maybe something else happened to him? Strange, before the

---

[14] Antanas Smetona, 1874-1944. President of Lithuania, 1919-1940, until its occupation by the Soviet government until the Molotov-Ribbentrop Pack. He was fervently anti-communist.
[15] International Organization for the Assistance of Fighters for the Revolution, established by the Soviet government to supply aid to underground communist members. .

war I never thought about stuff like this, that something might happen to somebody. But now with the war everything is so different...

Fewer cars are now driving along the street. I hear shots. We cannot wait any longer, we need to hurry to get to the railway station, to papa.

Each of us takes our bundle and we leave. We run from one yard to the next and at the final end we reach the railway station. But there is nothing good awaiting us here: a large crowd of people hurrying who knows where, people talking loudly and only bad news, that the last train left several hours ago. Someone adds that the train was bombed no sooner did it get outside the city. There will be no more trains.

We went to every corner of the train station, but we could not find papa anywhere. Only unfamiliar people forcing themselves in crowds on any person who was dressed in a railway uniform. They want a train, but the railway employees tell them that there are no more trains.

Some still hope that a train will be available and will wait, others are getting ready to walk, maybe along the road an automobile will pick them up. Mama remembers that papa said something about an automobile. Let's go.

We joined with other people. The sun was hot overhead. I need to drink and it is hard for me to walk. But we did not get very far and we could still see the city. Ruvik asks to stop, he needs to rest. Mama takes his bundle from him, but this does not help any, he is complaining anyway. Mama is not strong enough to also carry a five-year-old boy in her arms. And Rayechka, even though two years older and a little more sturdy, is also whimpering. I want to rest so much also, but I keep quiet.

We sit. Others who are stronger pass us and keep going. After we rested for a while mama convinced the younger two to get up. We pushed forward. But not for long, they again asked to stop and rest.

We sit. This time we were not alone. Not far from us several other families were resting.

We all gather together and travel further. Automobiles overfilled with people pass us. They cannot take us, but they tell us to hurry as the German troops are very close to the city. But how are we to hurry?

What are we to do? Some count it better to keep walking: better to die from exhaustion or starvation that at the hands of the fascists. Others are convinced that the Germans are really not so bad...

The children want to return home. Miriam tells them they need to walk further. I am silent. The children are crying. Mama notices that many are returning and likewise turns back.

At home the yard keeper says that papa came, and he said to tell us that he is looking for a car. We are at home again. The rooms seem alien to us. Our hearts are empty. We walk from corner to corner, stand at the window. The whole area is lifeless, it seems empty homes are all that remain in the city. You do not even see a cat running along the street. Are we really the only ones here?

Empty buses line the boulevards. They were abandoned right where they were parked at the first air raid alarm. It is so strange that all of this occurred within just a day and a half.

Dead silence. It is broken only occasionally by the sound of a random gunshot, and then again quiet... Along the street, behind the Red Army troops, several cadets with white armbands are running. They are pillaging. Some of them are breaking the windows of stores and also the *Kazino* movie theater and dragging large boxes out of there. The steps of the pillagers are hard sounds in the background of the silence.

It is now dark. Mama locks the door but we are afraid to lay down to sleep. I don't even want to. But Ruvik and Rayechka and mama, still dressing, go into the office and lay on the sofa.

Miriam and I stand at the window looking at the dark walls of the tenement buildings.

What is going to happen? It seems to me that I am more afraid than any of them. Although mama is acting differently, absentmindedly. Only Miriam is her normal self.

It is almost midnight when we hear the sound of motorcycles along the street. The Germans!

It is dawn.[16] Tanks are arriving. Aliens! Many of them carry the banner with the dreadful, inscribed black spider – the fascist swastika.

The whole street is already filled with the cars of the German officers, their motorcycles, green uniforms and arrogant talk. It is so strange and spooky to look at these foreigners, strutting about our Vilnius as though they owned the place.

There was no need for us to have returned... And papa is still not here.

The German officers ordered a restaurant and cafe to be opened, but specifically with the notice, *Fur Juden Eintritt verboten.* We are the *Juden,* and the occupiers count us to be the worst of all the others: *Jews are forbidden to enter.* I need to get near and break the window and take the worthless notice and tear it up!

I am afraid to leave the apartment. It is apparent that we are not alone holed up. In the street there are only German cadets with their white armbands.

Miriam then convinces me that we need to go to school to get her certificates and our other documents, as they [the Germans] could destroy them. I am the one who needs to go. Me, the younger of us, no one will touch. But I am afraid and do not understand why this is so necessary. But mama supports Miriam. The documents are needed. And Miriam is

---

[16] June 24, 1941

already 17 years of age, they could stop her and ask for her identification. I need to go. For greater safety mama orders me to wear my school uniform and even my formal cap.

At the gates I look in every direction. So many Germans! And if it should enter the head of one of them to stop me? But fortunately they do not even notice me. With my heart shaking I walk along the street. I attempt to not look at anybody and am counting my steps. It is so hot for me wearing my formal wool uniform. I cross Gediminas St. I glance each way in an unpretentious manner. There are a whole lot of cars and soldiers. They have green or brown or black uniforms. One walked by me right under my nose. He was wearing an armband with a swastika on it.

Finally I reach the school. The place is in total disorder, dirty. While on the stairs a 12th grade classmate named Kaukorus stops me and says, "Why are you here? March out of here now!"

I ask him to let me through. But he grabs my formal cap from my head. "Get out! And don't stink up our school with your presence." I turn around and bump into my teacher Jonaitis. Afraid that he will also reprimand me I try to get around him. But the teacher stops me, gives me his hand to shake and asks my reason for coming. He accompanies me to the chancellery and helps me find the certificates and grades. He accompanies me back so that I would not encounter Kaukorus again. He promises to come to our home that evening.

He kept his word. Mama was surprised as he was a person little known to us, just a schoolteacher but was talking to us as if he was a close relative, and even offering to us his assistance.

The was a pogrom in Snipiskes.[17] Villains started a bonfire and forced the Rabbi and some bearded elders to attend. They ordered them to throw the Torah into the fire with their own hands, and which they stole from the synagogue. They forced

---

[17] A neighborhood in Vilnius on the north bank of the Neris River.

the elders to undress and they took them by the hands and forced them to dance around the bonfire and sing *Katusha*.[18] Then they would scorch them with the fire and pull out their beards, beat them up and again force them to dance.

Was this really true? It is really possible to ridicule people this way?

On Naugarduko St was another pogrom.[19]

Other than this the occupiers hung several men upside-down by their feet. Some reported that they attempted to evacuate into the center of the Soviet Union, but they could not and so returned.

So what if the yard keeper will betray us? No doubt he will guess as to why we left the building.

In the streets an order was posted, "Communists and *Komsomols*[20] are required to register. And if anybody knows any Communists, *Komsomols*, or Members of the MOPR, who are avoiding registration, this must be immediately reported to the Gestapo."

I am a Pioneer.[21] But there was nothing said about the Pioneers in the directive. Mama says that they will nevertheless not force me to register. But I still had to wear my Pioneer neckerchief on occasion to certain events. Maybe I could discolor it by rubbing soot on it? No way! They gave it to me at school in a ceremony and tied it on me and I gave my promise to wear it. So now to dirty it? No way. We agreed to sew it inside one of my father's jackets under the lining. While mama was sewing, I played with the children so they would not see. Since they were small they might blurt it out.

Mama hid papa's badge indicating he was a member of the MOPR in the attic. She ordered us to review all of papa's

---

18 A popular Russian song.
19 In central Vilnius, where the main museum, university, library and cultural center are now located.
20 Young Communists League
21 Communist group for teenagers similar to the Girl or Boy Scouts.

business matters, especially those dealing with defending underground communists. If they find these documents, they will shoot us.

Among other things there were all sorts of business matters and even some interesting books. These I placed off to the side, hiding them carefully, then I would peruse them a second time.

One more announcement was posted in the streets, "The city must maintain order and calm. To secure this 100 men are taken as surety. In the event of the smallest amount of disorder or disobedience, all the hostages will be shot."

The occupiers were conducting themselves in a manner to indicate their intention of a long term stay. They introduced their own money – the mark. They were kind enough to allow the use of Soviet rubles, but then instituted an exchange rate of one ruble to 10 pfennings. This meant that 10 rubles was just worth one mark.

They hung a new order, "Other than Germans and *Volksdeutsche*, all are ordered to turn in their radio receivers. For any attempt to hide them or listen to Soviet or foreign broadcasts, the penalty is death." Mama and Miriam wrapped the radio in a towel and took it to them.

On the table that was now spared of the radio I placed my small album of verses, diary, pencils, and my inkwell. Now I had my personal desk just like the adults.

After a few days German officers went apartment to apartment to determine if the orders were being followed. Yesterday there were at our home. Not finding a radio receiver they confiscated papa's typewriter and telephone. They also confiscated the neighbor's telephone, bicycles and sewing machine.

Gayubene came to visit us today. She said that Salomeya Neris[22] fled to the Russians. She said that she could have lived peacefully if she was only to write poetry and not intervene into politics. Gayubene told us that she convinced the poetess not to express her approval of Lithuania's entrance into the Soviet Union, and not to go to Moscow as a delegate.[23]

I always thought that Gayubene was an extraordinary person, since she was friends with such a famous poetess as Salomeya Neris. But now I see that I was mistaken. Gayubene obvious only loved to associate with popular people. With the same arrogance she told us that she had a German officer living with her! Among other things, he wanted to buy some natural coffee. In Germany such coffee had not been available for a long while. He also wanted to buy a collection of Heine's poems.[24] In Germany Heine was forbidden (I guess he was also a *Jude*). Gayubene's houseguest considered him the best poet and wanted a collection of his poems.

Mama gave her some coffee and a volume of Heine. Gayubene promised to pay for it later.

The Germans again started to go to each Jewish apartment. Sometimes just them, sometimes they would also bring the yard keepers. They make a list of the furniture in each residence. Leaving they would give strict warning for everything to remain in their place: nothing was to be moved or sold. Even if one chair was to disappear they would shoot the entire family.

But if they were to see an especially nice sofa, they would take it and not even make a record of it. The pillagers!

---

[22] Salomeya Neris, 1904-1945, Lithuanian poet.
[23] Nevertheless, Neris was a delegate and even wrote a poem to the credit of Joseph Stalin, for which she received the Stalin prize.
[24] Johann Heinrich Heine, 1797-1856. German poet. He was originally Jewish but converted to Lutheranism in 1825. He moved to Paris in 1831, where he spent the remaining 25 years of his life.

Two weeks did not even pass from the start of occupation and all had changed.

Again new announcements were posted in the city, "All *Juden*, adults and children are required to wear a badge. It will be 10 centimeters square[25] made of white material with a yellow edge. In the center of the badge will be the letter *J*. These badges will need to be sewn on your outer clothing, to be located on the chest and also on the back."

The occupiers do not even count us as humans, as we are branded like cattle. There is no way possible under any circumstance to disagree with this. Will no one be bold enough to oppose it?

Mama orders us to discuss less and help her sew these badges. She cuts some yellow trim from an old bedspread and we get to work. A few neighbors come to our apartment, as they do not have any yellow cloth.

The work is clumsy. Either too wide or else it is crooked. No one is talking.

While leaving one neighbor announces that we should wear these badges with pride. She found something to boast about: a brand. I have no intentions of walking into the street with them. It is an embarrassment to meet a teacher or even a friend wearing them.

Then there was another demand of the German officers. All *Juden* were required to hand over all their money, jewelry, gold articles, and other valuables. Only 30 marks, which was 300 rubles, was allowed to be kept for ourselves.

Those bloodsuckers! Obviously some kind of devil must be sitting inside their cursed Gestapo office, and who devises new cruelties especially for us.

Badges and now the confiscation of money, but these were the least of the cruelties they would impose on us. They kill the innocent! Armed patrols restrain men in the streets and take

---

[25] 2-1/2 inches

them to the Lukiskes Prison.[26] Men are afraid to go into the street. But this would not save them anyway, as gangsters would break into houses at night and arrest even teenagers.

Initially everyone believed that the arrested were taken from the prison to Ponary, a work camp. But now we know that there was no work camp of any type at Ponary. They were shot there! Only cement-lined basins were there, and where they would discard the corpses.

This cannot be happening! This is so terrifying!!! Why? Why are they being killed?

They were called *Extortionists*,[27] and they never stopped with their ruthless cruelty. Each apartment built some kind of secret enclosure where the men could hide day and night.

Maybe it wasn't so bad that papa was not here. Maybe he was there, warring on the front to liberate us. When the teacher Jonaitis informs us about the news on Moscow radio (he did not give up his radio but hid it in a wood shed) all of it seemed to me that he was telling us something about papa. But every time this would cause mama to get scared. She of course also wanted to get information about papa, but not through the radio, because otherwise they would then shoot us because a member of our family was in the Red Army.

But perhaps they will not be shot? Some families of Soviet officers live nearby. They are locked in two buildings along Subachayus St and held there against their will. Of course no one knows what will happen to them later. In general you will not understand the Germans. In all the world prisoners-of-war are not executed, but they have already shot 4,000 at Ponary.

Shot... This means that these people were herded into a pit. The barrel of a machine gun was pointed at each of them and out of which a small bullet flew, penetrating the heart, and

---

[26] Located in central Vilnius.

[27] The Russian word Хапун, *khapun*, also refers to a type of bogeyman in Lithuanian mythology who would fly over the city and sweep away disobedient children and take them to his home, so did this appellation refer to the German soldiers who would arrest Jews and take them to Ponary.

these people fell down dead. No, not each bullet found its way to enter the heart or head, many were only wounded and they perished under horrible anguish. Thousands of lives were shredded, no more did so many joyous young men exist, but all of this was referred to by one word: execution. Earlier I did not comprehend the meaning of this word. Even fascism, war, occupation, seemed to me only words in some history textbook.

And now for sure people of other cities and countries, where there is no war or fascism, also do not comprehend, cannot imagine the genuine meaning of these words. This is why it is necessary for me to inscribe into a diary all that is occurring here. If I remain alive, I will talk about it personally, if not, others will read about it. But let them know! Absolutely!

More news. New badges are now being imposed on us. Not a square, but a white band and a six-pointed star will be in the center of it. The band must be worn on the left arm.

I want to eat all the time. Miriam and I talk about this only between ourselves in order not to embitter mama, while the youngsters are always complaining. Mama endures it all, she divides the bread into portions and often skips herself or takes the smallest portion. This is because with our ration cards they provide us very little and what makes it more difficult for us especially is not having decent access to a grocery store. The wait in line is immense. Often after standing an entire day people return home empty-handed as all the food is gone. Sometimes we eat what mama is successful in getting from the peasants. I yearn for milk so much.

One day the teacher Jonaitis brought a piece of fat. Confused, it took him a long while to explain how he got it with his ration card, but he did not need it. An adult can go without fat, but we have youngsters. Fat is so necessary for a growing organism. Mama is devastated and for me it is embarrassing that people are giving us charity. But the teacher insisted on it.

For dinner each of the youngsters got a piece of fat, while we were able to dine on some dry biscuits and potatoes.

But the good mood of a tasty dinner was blemished with bad news: a directive was issued at school that all the *Komsomols* – meaning Yu. Tityus, A. Titule, and others – and all the Jews were expelled from school.

This meant that I was no longer a student... What am I going to do all winter? So am I going to remain a half-educated person?

Miriam and I agreed on taking turns sleeping on the balcony that overlooked the yard. This is because our apartment, and especially the bedroom, is located opposite from where the gates are, and we never can hear if "nighttime guests" are knocking. We wake up only when they are already inside the yard. If we sleep on the balcony we can immediately hear them.

I begin my nighttime sentry duty. The night is warm. There are an infinite number of starts in the sky, and all of them are flashing. Now I will always sleep here, it is so nice. But am I really able to record all of this? Niole and Birute boast of my poetry, but they do not understand them any more than I do. But Luda praises them. But she writes some of her own.

> Oh – go – go.
> There in Limpopo[28]
> Lived an aged Don Juan
> A crocodile from the Nile.
> And if I were to record it all this night?
> The small stars flicker,
> They stare at me amazingly from their heights.
> Do they see how people here suffer
> And how the nights are so scary for them?

---

28 The northernmost province of South Africa, bordering Zimbabwe, Botswana and Mozambique. The poem rhymes in Russian.

This is poorly composed. Tomorrow I will sit and think this over carefully so that my poetry composition will be definitely contemporary. I need to listen to the respiration of the night. But it would be so much better without war. Is it proper to include terror in poetry? It is much better to write about autumn, about a joyful brook.

They are knocking! At our gates!!!

I run into the bedroom, I wake mama. Together with Miriam we help the children dress. Ruvik wants to complain, but then immediately stops, he understands that he should not.

They are already pounding on our door with their fists! Mama is going to open it. We follow after her.

Armed Gestapo tumble into our living room. They spread out into all the rooms. One stands to guard us. He orders us not to make a move or else he will shoot us.

They are digging in the cupboards, rummaging in boxes. They interrogate us, where is papa. Mama says that he was arrested the initial days of the occupation, right after hostages were taken. "Not true!" shouted the officer, the most evil there ever was one. "He most likely ran off with the Bolsheviks! All of you are Bolsheviks and soon it will be *kaput* for all of you!"

And again they search, throw items, scatter stuff. Mama is shaking and quietly tells us to watch them carefully so they do not claim they found a weapon or some illegal literature. They pretend they found something and act like they are shooting us. But how are we to follow their search if we are not allowed to even stir?

Not finding anything they once more threaten us, that soon it will be *kaput* for us. The Gestapo assemble and leave.

We still do not lay down. Mama cannot get the Gestapo officer's words that papa, no doubt, joined the Bolsheviks, out of her head. Maybe they know something? Maybe this is true, papa is there, alive and fighting!

I am no longer going to sleep on the balcony. I will tell no one of the verses and stars...

At the *Gebietskommissar*[29] they summoned the members of the *Judenrat,* which is the council of Jewish elders. (This council was created just recently out of the higher levels of the Jews of the city. The people who associated with Germans in the past felt that the German occupation officers would be able to deal this group.)[30] So what happened was that they told the *Judenrat* that the Jews of the city Vilnius have an obligation toward the contribution of five million rubles. This amount of money had to be brought to them by 9 o'clock of the following day. It this did not happen, then beginning at half-past 10, the annihilation of all the Jews of the city would begin. The designated sum could be brought not only in cash, but also its equivalent in gold, silver and other jewelry.

Mama gathered all of our money, took rings and chains and left.

I stand in the kitchen at the window and weep. It is horrifying to think that tomorrow I will need to die. It seems that just yesterday I was running through the corridors, answered questions in class, and all of a sudden I will die! I do not want to! I have lived so little! And I have not bid farewell to anybody. Even with papa. The last time I saw him was when we left the shelter, from the basement of the house opposite to us. I will not see him again. In general I will not see or feel anything anymore. I will not be any more. And all that is remaining will remain – the streets and meadows, even the lessons... It is only I who will not be there – not at home, not in the street, not at school... And do not look for me as you will not find me anywhere... And perhaps no one will even bother to look for me? They will forget about me. Isn't it like this, that I am an individual just for myself and for my close associates, but in general among the thousands of people I am a grain of

---

[29] German administration of occupied territories during World War 2.
[30] From another aspect, the German occupation required Jews to form a committee within their community or ghetto and which would deal with the Germans.

sand, one of many. Regarding myself, my aspirations and dreams, perhaps, someone at some time will recollect me with one word – she was. She was and perished one summer day when people could not gather the contribution demanded by the occupiers. And perhaps these circumstances will also be forgotten. It seems the living do not care to often remember the dead. Will this dead person be me?

Someone is walking along the corridor... It is the teacher Jonaitis. And I did not even hear him walk in. We stood next to each other and he placed his hand on my shoulder and was silent. But I could not seem to calm myself.

Mama returned. She let us know that at the office of the *Judenrat* they will wait for the results of sum of money. There is an immense crowd there.

Jonaitis opened his envelope and asked mama to take his money there also. But mama would not take it; it was 400 rubles, probably his income for teaching. But Jonaitis is waving with his hands, he will somehow survive, while this money perhaps will save at least one human life.

Mama soon returned. Everybody left the premises, she could not find out anything, the money was not yet counted, and we could only go there up to 8 o'clock. (Among other things we were the exception here also, because the balance of the city's residents could go there as late as 10 o'clock.) The members of the *Judenrat* will count the money the entire night. It just seems that the amount will not reach five million.

This was the final night... Jonaitis remains to spend the night with us. Mama is making a bed for him in the office, while we as usual will sleep in the bedroom.

The youngsters have fallen asleep. It is good that they do not understand anything. The night stretches so slowly, and let it. If time was to just somehow and immediately stop, then morning would not arrive and we would not have to die.

But the dawn did arrive...

Mama runs to the *Judenrat*. Of course she did not even reach their office. But people told her that there was a total of three and-a-half million that was gathered and they just took it to the *Gebietskommissar*.

Will they allow us more time? Perhaps not everybody knew about it yesterday and they will bring it today?

Mama gives each of us a bundle filled with clothes.

We wait...

The steps of the engineer Fried could be heard on the staircase (he lives in the apartment next door and is one of the members of the *Judenrat*.) Mama knocks on his door. She returned filled with joy, the occupiers accepted the contribution without even counting the amount.

This means we will live!

Everyone is hiding their valuables at the homes of the Lithuanians and Poles they know. The Germans can also document them just as they documented our furniture. Then we will have nothing to live on.

Mama took almost all of papa's books, jacket, suits, shoes, and two new silk blankets to the teacher Jonaitis' home. She decided that was enough. The teacher is a bachelor, and if they find any women's or children's articles in his possession they will suspect something. I included among the books the first notebook containing my memoirs.

People are looking for work because those who are working get a document with the German eagle on it, and the *Extortionists* are not supposed to bother them.

Many are working on fixing the streets, at the airport and other places. But it seems that this is hardly helping at all. Pillagers steal the documents and tear them up and still confiscate property.

They are so arbitrary, and there is no one to whom we can complain, and we cannot resist them. One woman would not allow them to arrest her husband, they shot her right on the spot and in front of his eyes.

Today is July 21. One month since the start of the war and my birthday. I am 14 years of age. Mama started to weep as she congratulated me and wished me many more years. How many times I heard this customary wish and not once did I ever turn my attention to how significant a statement it really was.

On the occasion of my birthday mama proposed that I wear my blue silk dress. It did not have the badges. I had such an unusually beautiful appearance! What was sad was that my hair was too long.

Suddenly this exciting thought entered my head. I asked mama if I could show my dress to the neighbor, Aunt Bertie. But at the same time I put my hand in a dresser drawer where some money was hidden under some linen, and then I slipped out the door. Mama started to cry afterward as if sensing a premonition that I would actually take the risk of going into the street without the badges.

But this is exactly what I was planning to do. I hurriedly jumped down the stairs and ran out the gates and bravely, not even looking around myself, turned onto Bolshoi St. I entered the hairdressing salon. Only now did I start to shake. What did I do?

They invited me to sit. I attempt to appear calm and not to look at the hairdresser. But he, wrapping a white towel around himself, smiles at me in the mirror. He noticed! I watch him and his eyes spread wide open, but I do not know how to make an expression pretending that I do not understand what is occurring. I drop my head so he cannot see my face. My heart is beating alarmingly, while the hairdresser, to spite me, is digging in the drawer. Maybe I should run? No need to... As long as some German officer does not enter!

Finally he finishes cutting my hair! I pay him and run.

I skip on my return trip. Now I am completely calm, and I do not even remember why I shook so hard at the hairdresser's. No one was bothering to look at me.

Mama set me straight. I had to promise to her that I would never again repeat such a stupid stunt. Mama sewed badges on all my dresses.

We are forbidden to walk on the sidewalks. We need to walk on the pavement holding to the right side. Among other things we are not to drive or ride in an automobile or bus, and etc. Even taxi drivers are required to place a sign in a visible spot that they do not offer service to Jews.

Again they introduced other badges. The star that was already on the armband was now to be moved. It was to be drawn on a square piece of white cloth and sewn to the top of our outer garment, both on the front and back.

I had to think about this. So what kind of German was this who does not want to himself serve at the front and so with his endless ideas he attempts to prove that he is very needed here.

The Gestapo again summoned the members of the *Judenrat*. Now what are they devising? Could it be one more contribution?

In great anxiety we wait for the neighbor. He retuned just before evening.

What occurred was that he and one other member of the *Judenrat* were released, but the balance were arrested. Why? What did the others do that was improper, and why were just these two released?

It was a hot August Sunday.[31]

About noon we heard noise.

We ran to the window. Drunken German soldiers were beating on a black-haired young man. They chased him to the

---

[31] August 31, 1941

town hall and then forced him to turn his face to the wall and were beating him. But he apparently was waiting to get shot as he was shaking all over.

A crowd gathered. One fascist announced that this *Jude* was just on Gediminas St and shot at an honorable soldier of the *Wehrmacht*.[32] "All the *Juden* will answer for this. One soldier of the great Reich is worth more than a thousand of this type. Let every person who wants to, beat this criminal and so join with us in the destruction of the enemies of the German nation."

Some grinned, satisfied at the situation, others continued to walk by and almost not hiding their agitation.

The German soldiers stop an automobile driving by, shove their blood-drenched sacrifice into it, and drive off.

We were shocked and petrified at the window.

Night...

A shot broke the silence. Someone shouted. They are running. They cry, "Halt!"

We wake the youngsters. My heart maintains a strange pain. I shake as though in a delirium. Again another sound of a shot. Cries, footsteps of a crowd. Many people, very many.

We open the shutters. Nothing can be seen. It is a cool star-filled night. Quiet. Somewhere off to the side toward the direction of the railway station a steam locomotive is whistling. And again not a sound... It was as if nothing had occurred.

Mama puts the children to sleep. We sit...

A terrifying cry suddenly interrupts the silence. Is it starting again? The voices seem to be somewhere next to us, very close. But mama decides not to go to the window, it is obvious why. Something inside of me pulls me, not knowing is more terrifying. I stand behind the curtain and look outside. Below in the street German soldiers are arranging people forced there from Mesinu St.

---

[32] The German military.

Sobbing women with their half-dressed children wrapped in blankets. Men hunched over due to their heavy bundles and suitcases. Children clinging to the clothing of adults. They are being pushed, beaten, driven. A pocket flashlight turns on and illuminates the frightened faces. The flashlight turns off and again all I can see are silhouettes moving.

So far it seems they are not knocking at our gates, although within a moment they can easily be already walking up the stairs.

They were taken away... It is quiet again.[33]

It is starting to light with the dawn.

It is apparent that during the night all the resident of Mesinu, Ashmenos, Disnos, Shyaoulu, Strashuno Streets and some others, were herded away.

People are saying that they are relocating the Lithuanians and Poles from these streets. That area will become our ghetto.

What is a ghetto? How do people live there?

On Friday evening patrols barricaded the city.

Something else they thought of... Like spite against us. Jonaitis did not arrive that day. Mama would have asked him to spend the night with us.

I gained the courage to go and invite him. Mama waved her hand, it was already 8 o'clock. I tell her, I will go without my badge. But she does not want to hear me. But there is no other way for me to deal with this. I will go.

It is not scary for me. Would it actually enter someone's head that at this time of the evening some Jewish girl would be skipping down the sidewalk without badges?

It is Gelezhinkelu St. I look around to see if anyone is following me. I enter. I knock. Quiet. I knock harder. No answer. He is not here! What should I do?

I need to wait.

---

[33] September 2, 1941; 3,700 were arrested that night.

47

I hide in the corner, outside the door. I catch every sound emanating from the street. I become petrified at every step of some boot, but at the calm shuffle of some girl's slippers my heart cheerfully pulses. But the footsteps get nearer and then fade into the distance, but no Jonaitis. How can I stand here the entire night? Someone will notice me. And mama will be annoyed.

Suddenly Jonaitis appears!

Finding out why I came, he is very bitter. It is already five minutes to 9 o'clock. We cannot go.

He lays me on the sofa, closes the shudders and orders me to sleep. But I cannot fall asleep. I am very upset because mama does not know where I am.

Once awakened I did not immediately recognize where I was. Jonaitis is leaning over me. "I will go and find out what the news is. Meanwhile cover yourself and sleep a little longer."

He returned rather quickly. He was not able to get to my home. They did not allow him. On Rudninka St there is a barricade. That is the location of the ghetto. People are already being herded into it.[34]

He asks me, "What are you going to do?"

"I don't know. How bad is the situation?"

He doesn't know either. "If you don't want to leave, stay with me."

So how am I to live alone, without mama? No. I will go.

Jonaitis empties his briefcase and puts some dried cheese and a can of jam in it. He empties a folder and says, "Hide this well." Out of some yellow paper we cut some badges, we sew them on. "Right now you cannot get by without them."

We leave. Jonaitis likewise takes the street walking along the pavement, he does not want me to feel humiliated. If I was to close my eyes, would I feel I was walking to school? It seemed that way: briefcase, school uniform, and my teacher next to me. No, I do not need to close my eyes.

---

[34] September 6, 1941

On Rudninka St, near the Catholic Church, barricades are being assembled. Soldiers are herding people through one remaining passage. We walk toward it. Jonaitis cheerfully clasps my hand and I pass through the barricade.

Where do I go? Maybe I should attempt to go home? They will not allow me. All around me are barricades.

New and more new people are being herded in. Disheveled, tired. They toss their bundles from themselves and sit on them, right in the street, in yards. The place is everywhere filled with this crowd. I am going in circles. Finally I enter our yard, but mama is nowhere to be found and I do not see anyone familiar.

I stand at the entrance to our building to see the new people being herded. I ask from what street they are. They name all the streets, but none of them is mine. Some woman tells me that everyone from Nemetski St was herded to Lidski St. I run there. But they are building a new barricade there. This street remains outside the limits of the ghetto. Many people are there, but my family is not among them.

Again I start to wander, lost, I am asking this person and that person. Someone supposes that they might be at the second ghetto, somewhere in the area of Stiklu and Gaono Streets.

I walk to the gates and ask the sentry to permit me. I assure him that I will not run away, but only want access to enter the second ghetto where my mother is. But the sentry acts as if he is not even listening. I repeat my request again, but then he waves his hand and strikes me so hard that I was barely able to stand on my feet. Unexpectedly I notice one classmate from the 9th grade in my school. He holds a machine gun, likewise also performing his duty. As politely as I possibly could I ask for his help to cross into the second ghetto. "Go!" he hollers.

I enter. He leads me, walking behind me with his gun almost right in my back as though I was under arrest. Let him. We get near Stiklu St. The barricade is already rather high.

"Can you climb over it?" I quickly answer, "Yes, yes." He helps me climb over the barricade and I ease myself down on the other side.

Here the crowd is larger and more disorderly. The yards are smaller and darker. So many people, but again none from our street. It is as if all the residents of Nemetski St just disappeared underground.

From one yard I unexpectedly saw Aunt Prana. What is she doing here? I found out that she lives here, but she was now being moved into a different apartment, because this is where the ghetto will be located. All of her belongings were piled into a cart. I asked her to go to our home and if mama is still there to relate to her where I am.

Aunt Prana invited me to stay in her apartment. But why do I need an apartment? Well, I guess I will be living here. But how can I live without a bed and things? Aunt Prana left me one small stool. I sat and so did I sit in these empty rooms in someone else's home.

Some man quickly walks in. He looks around and calls for his family. An immense family enters – children with bundles, a baby carriage, small pillows, kitchenware. Not saying anything they occupied one room.

Others came. They occupied the room where I was. The closer to evening the more often different people would open the door and wander in. In just this room three families were shoved together, in the other were two families. They ordered me into the kitchen. I was by myself and there was room enough for another family. But I walked into the kitchen and it was already occupied with another family. I sat in the porch.

It became dark. Very stuffy. I am afraid to go outside. I remain completely without a place.

People are getting ready for bed. The parents give their coats and pillows to the children, while they lie directly on the floor. Some old man is complaining, there is more room for him in a grave.

I do not want to soil my school uniform, so I do not lie down. It is cold. My feet are starting to get numb. Those sitting in the rooms often go into the porch and touch me each time. The night is so long.

Finally the light.

Again I start wandering in the search for mama. Some suppose that my family is still in the first ghetto, others are sure that everyone from our street was hauled to prison. This cannot be, for me to remain alone, abandoned. I will find them!

And I again start to search.

It is already now dark. I enter some apartment building, I walk to the second floor and sit in a dark entrance on the floor. No one is turning their attention to me, no one is bothering me.

I put my briefcase under my head and lie down. My nose senses a pleasant and very familiar smell. It seems to be coming from the briefcase. How did I not guess this from the start, this is the smell of jam! And I had eaten nothing since yesterday morning!

I stick my hand in it. Broken glass! The jar broke. The entire inside of the briefcase was smeared with strawberries and sticky juice. Nevertheless it is still tasty. But I need to eat it carefully, so not to swallow any broken glass. I sit in the darkness and shove all of it into my mouth together: bread, fat, jam, cheese. After nothing is left I again lie down.

Once awake I go into the street. Handwritten announcements were hanging everywhere, "Ghetto police are being organized. Those who want to register must..." and etc.

Apparently they found enough to join. Some complainers no doubt, and now having this special armband they are pushing their weight around, acting like they are big shots.

I still cannot find my family, although I have traversed every yard and some several times. People advise me to cross into the first ghetto, maybe they are actually there. The

51

"government" at the same time is gathering those just like myself – displaced – and to remove them from the first ghetto.

There are a lot of us. The newly-created police force is assembling all of us, counting us and ordering us not to wander away. Then the police disappear themselves and do not reappear for a long while. Returning, they count us again. Finally they decide to take us somewhere. Along with them an armed regiment also accompanies us.

They do not open the door to the first ghetto for a long while. We stand and tremble in fear that they might herd us into prison. But the guards do not allow us to return where we were before.

Finally the gates opened and behind I see my mother smiling and alive! And Miriam! And the children! Apparently Aunt Prana kept her word and let them know where I was. And mama also knew about the transfer of all those who got lost in the shuffle.

There was no end to our joy and conversation. Now these days of solitude and search did not seem to have been so horrible.

But mama also lived through quite a bit.

That evening after waiting as long as she could for me and Jonaitis, she concluded that they recognized me and arrested me. She wept the entire night. And in the morning when she saw that barricades being built not too far away, she descended into total despair.

What happened is that Aunt Prana unexpectedly came, and mama decided to voluntarily enter the ghetto. At this time soldiers flooded our living room. They gave them five minutes to gather and take with them only as much as they could carry. Mama threw our coats and dresses into the children's tub, and from cushion covers made backpacks for herself and Miriam and packed them full of linen. She even gave each of the youngsters a backpack, bundle and briefcase and tied their shoes to them.

The hardest part of all was to leave. But the soldiers harassed her for being so slow. Realizing that threats were not helping, they pushed Rayechka and Ruvik toward the staircase. Mama ran after them. Only at the door they looked back once more.

Neighbors were already gathered in the yard, also loaded with bundles and winter coats. Someone said that there is no reason to bring a coat as the war will end before winter.

They herded them into Rudninka St, but mama was straining to enter the ghetto! And good that she is here. Those from our street that were gathered for the second ghetto were transferred to the Lukiskes Prison as both ghettos were already overfilled. And those assembled in Lidski Street were also taken to prison "for correction of errors." There were about 6,000 persons there. Only a few families of them all were released, those specialists that could be employed by the occupiers. Those liberated from prison described horrible things: the cells were so packed that it was impossible for everyone to sit. The entire time people stood clinging to one another. And you could not even talk about leaving for personal needs.

We live in the first building from the gates. Rudninka 16. Our apartment contains a few beds left here from its previous tenants. They are used by the aged and children. The five of us sleep on the floor in the area between the two windows. During the day all the blankets are stored, otherwise there is no passage. Even then, not everyone can fit on the floor. One girl sleeps on the table, while another in the tub. One family has made themselves comfortable in the kitchen. There are eight whole families living in our apartment.

Our sense of time little by little vanishes. The ghetto becomes familiar and almost part of us. This one is larger than the second. Here are the residents of more streets: Rudninka,

Mesinu, Strashuno, Shyaoulu, Disnos and Ligonines. The other one seems to only have Gaono, Zhidu and Stiklu Streets.

A large poster decorates the outside of the gates of our ghetto, "Attention! Jewish quarter! Danger of infection. Entrance to unauthorized people prohibited."

From its initial days an "authority" was formed in our ghetto: a police force and a new *Judenrat*, whose president was A. Fried, a member of the first *Judenrat*. Police stations were opened on Rudninka, Ligonines and Strashuno Streets. The commandant's office was located at Rudninka 6, in the former high school, along with the office of the new *Judenrat*. The chief of the ghetto police was Yakov Gens.[35] They say he was a former officer of the Smetonov era army, and later worked at the Kaunas prison.

The ghetto police apparently were needed in order to convey to us the directives of the authorities and to make sure that they were diligently observed. And these directives were issued one after another. First, it was necessary to give up all money and jewelry (and this did not occur just once), and only keep 300 rubles for yourself. Second, a person could be outdoors in the ghetto only until 7 o'clock in the evening, then the police go on duty, meaning, a restricted period. Third, everyone was obligated to continue working where they were working before they were relocated in the ghetto. However it was forbidden to go into the city on an individual basis. Those who worked at the same place were to travel there in an organized group, like in a team. Fourth, to walk without badges was categorically denied, whether in the ghetto or outside its boundaries. (Now this badge was a solid yellow star. All the corners of the star needed to be firmly sewn to clothing. One star on the front, another on the back.) Fifth, it was forbidden to indirectly access any city offices. All matters were to be decided through the commander of the ghetto police. And so forth and more similar.

---

[35] Yakov Gens, 1903-1943.

By order of the occupation an *Arbeitsamt* – Employment Exchange – was opened in the ghetto, which was responsible to register all the residents capable of working. So now if someone in the city needed workers from the ghetto, the employers could turn to the German *Arbeitsamt*, and which would in turn inform the ghetto *Arbeitsamt*, and finally send over a team.

Yakov Gens assigned his brother Soloman Gens as the commander of the ghetto *Arbeitsamt*, while the intermediary between the city and ghetto division of the Employment Exchange was someone named Braudo.

The workers were to receive an identification card called an *Ausweis*. In it was recorded that *der Jude* was (place available for personal name and surname) works (place available for the name of the company). A statement was also included that without the approval of the *Arbeitsamt*, they could not assign this Jew to work elsewhere.

Mama was also able to get work, at a sewing factory. This was so good as she has gold hands and was able to sew!

We receive food ration coupons. But we received unbelievably so few of them. Like one person said, "We will not die of hunger, but you can hardly call this life." Bread was 125 grams a day;[36] then the following produce per week: 80 grams of cereal,[37] 50 grams of sugar, 50 grams of sunflower seed oil, and 30 grams of salt. But we never received any sunflower seed oil or any sugar. They only gave us bread and black beans instead of grains.

The occupiers would not just short us on food, but also with paper. They introduced colored cards. A yellow card for one person; a red for two; a pink for three; a green for four.

The amount of produce that was received was insufficient, now each person would strive to bring something home as he was returning from work, sometimes selling clothes for food, or sometimes kind people would just give them some. But F.

---

[36] About 6 oz
[37] This would be barley, rice, corn or oats. About 3 oz.

Murer[38] from the *Gebietskommissar*[39] smelled this procedure going on and hung a new directive on the gates saying that it was strictly forbidden to bring food products and wood into the ghetto. The guards at the gate, which was composed of one city policeman and several ghetto policemen, were responsible for searching each person entering the ghetto. Anything they found was confiscated and the violator was arrested by German officers.

This meant that even if you wanted to bring a piece of bread into the ghetto you could pay for it with your life.

Today was the first day of lessons at school.[40] Although there was two weeks delay, but with our presence it was again starting. And here I was.

Apparently the bell already rang... All entered the class. The spot for my partner was vacant... And the spot where A.R.[41] sat was also vacant. And why? Because we are forbidden to attend school and have our lessons? Because we are captives here and not allowed to go into the city?

A few days earlier I spoke about this with A.R. We recollected school, our class. But now A.R. appeared completely different. His clothes were soiled, dirt under his nails. He was working but did not say where, and apparently was embarrassed. His hair was unusually short. Even his eyes were not the same, but were now dull looking.

Gens assigned to us a new directive from Murer: all artisans need to live in the first ghetto – meaning ours – while all the others in the second. On the worker's identification cards there is a special stamp for the artisans. If a person does not have

---

[38] Franz Murer, 1912-1994.
[39] Central administration of the occupied regions
[40] School inside the ghetto
[41] Aleksandr Ran, 1926-1944, a schoolmate of Masha's.

this stamp, he is required to move into the second ghetto, while the artisans living in that ghetto will be relocated here.

Fortunately this special stamp was printed on mama's identification card. She is considered a tailor, sewing something out of fur.

One man in our apartment was not identified as an artisan. The commander ordered him and his family to vacant the building and go into the yard and to take their belongings with them.

A rather large group of people were gathered there, all of them disappointed and dreary. I felt so sorry for them. They did not have enough time to adjust to one place and now they were herding to another.

They open the ghetto gates. The city police are waiting for them there. They are leading all of them out of there... [42]

The exodus of the non-artisans from our ghetto lasts for several days. The ghetto police go apartment to apartment at nights and check all identification cards. Those not having the necessary stamp are accompanied out and to the second ghetto.

There is no precise news about those evacuated. A few persons were able to get some scrawled messages through an intermediary, but they were not decipherable. While those relocated here from the second ghetto – and there were just a few of them – said that over the past few days not even one person was brought there.[43]

We hear nothing good about the war at the front. It is true that nothing of consequence evolved from Hitler's lightning war. They boasted that they will reach Moscow within two weeks. Then later they boasted just the same about the time being delayed somewhat, and then said they were already at Moscow's suburbs. But all of this are lies. They were stopped.

---

[42] September 15, 1941
[43] About 3,000 were evicted and taken instead to Ponary.

And of course they will never see Moscow. But they have renewed the invasion and Leningrad is surrounded. Nevertheless they will be defeated!

Yom Kippur.[44] Today this holiday is especially melancholy. The aged fast, pray, and ask for God's mercy. The effort is futile. If there were a God, he would not tolerate such terrors.

It is noon. Suddenly drunk soldiers rush into the ghetto. People are running in every direction, the streets are vacant. The German soldiers roam about as if they own the place, they look into the yards, threaten people, shoot into the air. Mama, Miriam and the other adults of our apartment are at work. What are we to do? Will they lead us away? It is possible. Since we do not work, they don't need us. The youngsters are staring at me with these eyes as though I know something or can save them... But what can I do? I am most afraid of us all. But I must not give them this impression, but instead calm them so they do not start crying. I wish mama would be home soon! Finally the soldiers leave. Mama gets home. It is now dark and we go to bed.

Through my sleep I heard some kind of noise. It is as though a car drove up. I jumped up and stepped over the others sleeping and walked to the window. Although it was walled up, like all the windows that faced the open streets,[45] through a small opening I could see the corner of the street near the gates.

Soldiers were jumping out of a truck that just drove up. They are assembling... Should I wake the others or not? Maybe, but not to scare them, but they do not seem to be going anywhere, they are arranged in formation.

It is quiet. The city is sleeping. The soldiers appear petrified, not making a move. Maybe they always increase the guard at nights? But the nights are dark, it is already autumn.

---

[44] The Day of Atonement, from Tuesday September 30 to Wednesday, October 1, 1941.
[45] The Germans walled the windows that faced outside the ghetto.

Again the hum of more cars. So many soldiers are in them!

Frightened I wake everybody. A horrible panic starts. The children are crying, mothers are sighing, no one can seem to find their clothes. I am turning in circles half-dressed, shaking from fear and cold. The soldiers are already knocking at our gates... They are already in the yard! They are walking up the stairs... They are knocking! No one is opening the door. Their pounding fists sound like a drum. Beating hard on it. Right now they will break the door apart.

A neighbor stealthily moves to the door and tells them that all the residents of this apartment were relocated to the second ghetto. No one else remains but he, an artisan at the *Kailis* factory. Of course, they do not believe him and order him to show his identification card. The neighbor shoves it through a slot in the door. The soldiers review it, fumble with it and with laughter shred it into pieces. Then they walk away and start knocking on the next apartment.

Again I slide to the window. The gates are opened. They are herding people out of the ghetto. Arranging them. They also have children holding bundles. Some man tries to run back. Then the sound of a gunshot...

The entire crowd is herded along Pilimo Street, and more are herded out of the ghetto. Again they are arranged...

Mama asks me not to look through the window, but I cannot stop. What is so terrifying is that maybe I will soon be standing there myself. Mama calms us, "They will not find us." The neighbor's son walks to the staircase and nails the door closed from the outside with boards, and then he climbs back into his apartment through a window. He figures the murderers will conclude that no one lives here.

But it did not make any difference and they are knocking! It is obvious they do not believe it... Right now they will break it down. No. They are laughing. Instead of looking for Jews to take to Ponary, they were beating at a mouse hole that had a board nailed over it.

They left.

They are leading one more large crowd out through the gates. The soldiers climb into the cars and drive away.

Again it is quiet. The street again slumbers. Up high, and where my eyes cannot reach through the crack, the moon is shining.[46] It is illuminating the land. And for sure also those who right now are hunched over, melancholy, sad. Are they thinking of fleeing? Surely they are. But this is impossible. There are too many guards, the streets are empty, the gates are locked.

Prison. The immense heavy gates open. They creak, discontent that they cannot even rest at night. The poor souls are herded in like cattle and they close.

Sunlight at dawn. Mama is getting ready for work. She orders us to remain in bed and sleep. But how can I fall asleep if I can clearly imagine how terrifying it is right now over there at the prison. People are living the last day of their life. There are many of them. In cells, corridors, even outside. Rain. And they are sitting on their bundles, holding their weeping children to their chests.

Mama returns from work.

... And those in prison are still sitting there.

Night. Soon they will lead them out.

By now no doubt they are being ordered to stand in some formation. They are pushed and beaten.

The gates open wide. They are releasing them on their final walk. Herded with whips the people walk, walk, not realizing how it will all end. There are many of them. The soldiers are already fed up with killing.

It has ended. The gates close. The sentries walk and check all the corners. Was anyone left behind? Strange, as it is also prohibited for anyone to remain in prison.

---

[46] Almost full-moon, which will occur on October 5, 1941

Rain is sprinkling. But the people are walking. Slowly, dragging their feet. It is a large funeral procession. People are burying themselves. But surely not all of them realize this.

In one window I can see a sleepy man. Steps on the empty street woke him. Once seeing the crowd he disappears. Maybe he is going back to sleep, wrapping himself in his soft blanket, burying himself in his warm pillow and falling asleep... Will his sleep be disturbed by the thought that right now and there at Ponary thousands – wet from the rain and blood – are falling into a clay pit? And this occurring while he is sweetly dreaming. They fall one on top of the other, with their hands thrown back, mowed down, their faces expressing fear and pain. Men collapsing on small children. Young women, teenagers, the aged, all together, all into one...

Will this enter the mind of this sleeping man? (But why is it that I so clearly imagine this?) Will it dawn on him that just a half-year ago, or even four months ago, all of these doomed to their death were teachers, workers, simple parents and children? They were humans!

But perhaps this person who showed himself at the window hid himself not due to indifference, but from pain? Perhaps he, just as with myself, is suffering much, he would like to help, but... Is it possible for one person to disperse this type of armed regiment and hide the entirety of this large crowd? He cannot. And so he suffers twice as much.

It appears that the teacher Jonaitis was near the ghetto last night. He heard of the terror of the previous night and was afraid that the German soldiers would continue their bloody activity. Together with some friends, and who were all able to get some passes for that night, he stood not far from the gates. If they were to arrest us, perhaps he might be able to save us somehow.

I registered at the library. This was the library formerly named the Strashuno, but now the shelves are so vacant. The Gestapo agents appropriated more or less all the valuable books, while the compositions of Soviet writers they just plainly incinerated. They made the threat that they will regularly inspect the library. If they find a book having some communist subject matter they will not just shoot the library employee, but also as many people as there are pages in this book.

The ghetto administration prohibits books in our apartments. All were required to give up any books we possessed to the library. The library workers had to make sure these books would not get lost. Just to read books an authorization was required from the ghetto police office.

There is a reading room. Narrow, tiny, but when there are so many families residing in one room, it is almost unthinkable to read at home. But I want to read so bad! Even for a short while to forget where I am.

An address bureau was annexed to the library. It was similar to a post office and we even had an address just like in a genuine city. All the addresses were recorded. They put this girl here to do it, and she sits, the poor thing, yawning all the while. The initial days we were there, someone would take advantage of the opportunity and ask about some relative who disappeared, but now, whoever is alive will make themselves known in this cramped area, and if someone does not, the address bureau will not search for him.

A.R. found out from someone about the latest news: Moscow is holding its ground! It is being heroically defended, and not only by the army, but by the local residents. Even students are helping, they are digging trenches. And we would enthusiastically help to dig trenches if we could, anything to all the sooner bring an end to Hitler.

They gave us inoculations against some kinds of infectious diseases. In general here, and to the extent that this is permitted, the ghetto doctors worry about the health of the residents.

At Building 11 on Rudninka St there is a medical emergency ward, while on Ligonines St there is even a hospital. Some rooms are designated for the sick that have infectious diseases. There is a small shed in the yard that houses the mentally ill. (But not too long ago it was filled with perfectly normal people!)

There is a morgue at the entrance to the hospital, and on the other side is a pharmacy. Of course, it does not look anything like a genuine one, it does not even smell like medicine. The only items you can buy there are the simplest powders.

At the pharmacy they accept prescriptions and requests for the sick, in the office next door they write passes to visit the sick. Without a pass you cannot even stick your nose inside. There is even a mean old man that sits at the entrance. In short, all of it is like a genuine hospital, except horribly meager.

For ghetto cleanliness a sanitation police corps was created. From early morning doctors and nurses would walk through the yards and apartments, verifying their cleanliness. Are the floors being moped? Is there dust under the beds (where there are beds)? And even inspecting the toilet. If the cleanliness does not meet their expectations, the residents are forced to comply.

The trample of heavy military boots again awakened us at night. We watch, at the gates there is a large regiment of German soldiers. They are getting dressed, but suddenly they hear the commander's voice to turn around. The officer shouted for the soldiers to walk to the second ghetto.

I can only imagine what is going to happen there today.

In one of the apartments where the noise awoke the residents, they are attempting to hide. They are pulling up the door in the floor that descends to the cellar. But at that very moment the murderers rush into the room.

On the table a small flame is consuming what is left of a candle. Disheveled beds and blankets, chairs upside down. The executioners are pillaging. Having removed their military jackets they are putting on suits, shoving shirts into their undershirts. When there is no more room to insert more they open the cellar door. They jump in. Their flashlights illuminate the damp walls and the faces frozen in fright. They order them to stand on their knees in front of them — the conquerors of Europe. They walk between those on their knees, laughing at them, hitting them on the back, barking at them. Having gotten their fill of the scene they chase them out.

In the street one of them attempts to run. The villains break his arms and drag him to the crowd, assuring him that if should continue to resist the only remedy is to transfer him to the work camp. But he kicks and bites them and finally breaks out of their clutches and runs. But a bullet catches up to him...

Someone in the crowd is mourning, there was no need for him to flee. Maybe they will indeed take them to this camp?

The dark October night accompanies them as they walk out of the city...

The second ghetto was completely liquidated that night. About 9,000 residents were there.[47]

At early morning not far from the entrance of our ghetto they found a woman who just delivered crawling from the other ghetto. She was not able to crawl wherever she was going and died in children birth in the street. The newborn was healthy and crying and she was brought into the ghetto. They named her — Ghetta.

Those who worked at the *Kailis* factory were removed from the ghetto. In the city, not far from the factory, they are creating a separate location for them. The are barricading the area, but

---

[47] This would be October 29, 1941

people seem to think that there will be no *aktion*[48] there. The director of the *Kailis* factory supposedly intervened and tried to make arrangements so none of his workers would be affected.[49]

Not everyone is being relocated there, as the place will not fit all the workers. The director anyway is soon getting a new residence, another one next door.

Although Gens announced that the residents of our ghetto, meaning the artisans, will not be threatened anymore, no one believes him, and this was probably just what German authorities told him. For several days now people have been talking about some kind of yellow identification cards. Kailisov already received one. The identification card is just like the white one, but a yellow color and it is not called an *Ausweis*, but a *Facharbeitern*[50] *Ausweis*. Only the good artisans receive one, and not even all of them, because there are only 3,000 of the new cards issued, while there are a total of 10,000 workers. For the members of the *Judenrat* and the ghetto police they issued 400 identification cards. The conclusion is that almost all of them get one, even though they are not artisans, but from among the artisans only about a quarter of them get one.[51]

Mama got one! Of the 230 working at the sewing factory, only 80 of these new identification cards were issued.

Much unrest in the ghetto. Nothing definite, but all are talking that no one should go to bed tonight.[52]

Late that evening we found out that all those who possess a yellow identification card are required to registered at the *Judenrat*. The registration will occur the entire night, up to 4 o'clock in the morning. Each person with this card needs to show with the members of his family – husband or wife and

48 action, operation or campaign
49 This would be October 5, 1941
50 Qualified worker
51 This would be October 23, 1941
52 This would be night of November 3-4, 1941.

children up to 16 years of age. Children older than 16, other parents, brothers and sisters, will not be registered. Of course only the ghetto police and those who work at shops maintained by the Gestapo are excluded.

What a good thing it is that Miriam also received a new identification card, as she is already 17 years of age.

Early morning the next day all those who had a yellow identification card were required to go to work and take with them those members of the family that registered. They were to return to the ghetto only during the evening of the following day.[53] Those who did not receive the new identification card and their families were to remain in the ghetto.

Very frightening. The mood was heavy. People were mean, nervous, all deliriously hurrying to register. If someone did not have a new identification card they would look to join someone else or at least have them register their children as their own and so save them. Now those who had new identification cards suddenly inherited new relatives and especially children. Some brothers registered their sister as their wife, some widowers passed off their older daughter as their wife...

We are also going to register. People are trudging along the dark streets. All are moving in the same direction. Some of them have candle stubs lit, holding them in one hand and covered with their other palm, on occasion another will light a match. It is as dark as sitting inside a bag. Someone lost their child. She runs back scared and calls for him.

Judenrat. The wide staircase of a former high school is packed with people. All are aiming for the upstairs, to the tables offering salvation. Those finished and descending knock against the crowd with their elbows. The majority are sobbing: they did not register one mother, another was a 17-year old son. The ghetto police are trying to keep order, but the crowd does not pay attention to them. The one who feels death so close to him does not feel getting hit.

---

[53] This would be the evening of November 5, 1941

Noise, chaos, no one seems to believe that just a half-year ago students were walking up and down this staircase. A skeleton hangs in a former classroom, as if observing all of them, those who are right now struggling with death. The maps and chalkboard are at rest. In the corner a pile of some kind of decorations are scattered, ballet costumes. But it seems that no one is noticing them. Even I have myself forgotten that such things exist. Strange, it seems to a person that the whole world changes as his life does...

We can see the registration tables. Some man is having a conversation with mama. He is asking mama to register him as her husband. Mama is scared. But he is fervently trying to convince her to do this, that this will not affect us, while it will save his life. He begs her not to refuse. He asks us our names, the years all of us were born, what he should call himself, he tells her where he works.

Mama hands the registration certificate. He looks at us, records the information and hands mama small blue cards with a number on each.

The eyes of this man so greedily shined when he saw his ticket to salvation! He creates a way for us to leave and does not stop with his gratitude. It even became uneasy to have to listen to such exciting words. What has happened to people? Just for a decent and regular humane act he thanks us as if we accomplished something for him that was extraordinary, heroic.

We returned home. There are 17 persons in our apartment who do not have a new identification card or ticket. They will remain here. But some of them were able to register their children with other people. Now the parents need to bid farewell to them... The children are sobbing, they do not want to leave without their mother, and they through their tears greedily kiss the familiar face and hands and painfully whisper, "Go with uncle and aunt, listen to them. They will save you." But who really knows if it will be this way?

The light of sunrise. We are already in the yard and await mama's ascribed husband, without a yellow card but now with his inaccurate blue ticket.

We exit the yard. The barricades are holding back a large crowd. Murer and other officers are carefully verifying identification cards, inspecting each member of the family. They are routing the "culls," meaning anyone suspected of being older, into the fenced yard of the neighboring building.

A girl is walking toward the exit. She has her aged parents by the hand. Murer takes her identification card, orders her to pass, but pushes her parents into the area of the "culls." But the girl continues to pull them in her direction. Murer is resisting. She grabs her identification card out of his hand and nevertheless leads her parents. Murer throws her against the wall and takes his pistol...

When I open my eyes she is lying still... Murer calmly returns to his previous spot and continues verifying cards.

Finally we also exit. Along with a large group of people we are walking to the *Kailis* unit. But now they do not allow us to enter; it is already overfilled. Men are somehow trying to convince them to at least let us go into a garage. We sit on our bundles at the gates. Those working there just continue on their business.

Drizzling rain.

It is already night. Our feet are numb. I so much want to stretch them and even for a minute to somewhere lay my head.

It is now dark. The rain is harder now. It will soon be midnight. How intolerably difficult. When will all of this end?

Pious persons assure us that the ground does not want to accept innocent sacrifices and throws them back. This is why hands penetrate from the ground... But as mama explained, it is even simpler: the majority of those shot lay in the pit wounded. They eventually die and then swell. There are so many of them that they cause the surface of the soil that is used to cover them to burst. So in the cracks hands and feet and heads can be seen.

This is why the pits are not filled to the top, but the bodies are covered first with quicklime.

Horrible thoughts circulate in my head, not even allowing me to doze, although this is the second night without sleep and my eyes are sleeping on their own.

Finally the dawn we have awaited. Mama and the others workers again leave.

Now we await evening when we can return home.[54] The autumn days are short, soon it will start to become dark. But no one seems to be in a hurry, it is frightening. Maybe they have not yet finished their *aktion*?

Finally we decide to return.

The ghetto retains a spooky emptiness. Discarded bundles are scattered in the streets. Wide opened doors display the darkness inside. Under our feet the fragments of broken glass crackle.

Our apartment is empty. Those 17 persons are not here. Stuff is covered with white fluff, like snow. The pillagers shredded the pillows.

What is next?

The occupiers are getting more insane. It is obvious because they are not being sent to the front.

It is so much harder now to escape from the ghetto. The populace is scared, they are afraid to even hide. Murer's latest directive is printed in the newspapers, "If any hidden Jews are to be found at someone's residence, the most severe punishment will be imposed on the residents of the apartment." Most severe punishment meant hanging. I heard that as a warning several city residents were already hanged in Kafedralnoi, Ratushshi and Lukiskes squares.

---

[54] This would be the evening of November 5, 1941

If a person is able he attempts to at least leave to the surrounding localities. They say it is calmer there.

People are selling the last of their rags and renting trucks. Children are carried in knapsacks or led by the hand and attired in adult clothing. After work they do not return to the ghetto and once darkness descends they wait at some designated place.

But so far very few have been able to attain the goal of escape. They are caught somewhere along the road.

Is there no salvation?

The people arrested during the *aktion* of the previous week seem to still be alive, but this is occurring again...

This time those who carry a yellow identification card are required to leave with their families, not just for one day, but for three.

One person we know, Aunt Rosa, decided not to hide. She says that they will find her within three days anyway. And if this time she should by miracle survive, then for sure she will be captured the next round, eventually everyone will be killed. This is their agenda...

It is spooky for me to listen to her. But mama is angry at her. How can she agree to die? To sit and wait until they come for her!

The neighboring apartment is filled with a feverish upheaval: they are preparing for an escape. The are bringing bundles full of linen, hunks of bread, pots filled with cooked black beans. People are entering. With caution they stare at the neighbor with the small child: will he start crying? This is not the first time that a secret was exposed due to a child's cry.

A young man and his sister, whom he ascribed in the identification card as his wife, hide their parents. The doors to the room are masked by covering it with an immense antique buffet. They nail it to the wall. They arrange dishes all over the apartment floor and especially bottles of vodka that they had been hiding until now and for such an occasion.

If the executioners come, the vodka will distract their attention.

These three days pass.

We are back in the ghetto. The first thing I do is run to the neighboring apartment. How did the clandestine operation go? It failed... They moved the buffet over. This means the child nevertheless started to cry. A normal occurrence caused the attempt to fail. This happened just as with many other attempts...

... The first day. It was quiet in the room, day. The child sleeps. The soldiers enter the apartment, search for a while and leave. Distance sounds can be heard from the street, occasional separate gunshots. But it seems that it is safe in the room.

Nighttime. Mother wakes the child and quietly plays with her, feeds it, anything so it does not sleep. Let him sleep during the day. But as usual his eyes closed and he falls asleep. What will happen during the day?

Morning. Again soldiers arrive. Today they search the premises more carefully. But the child is not sleeping. He is adjusted to the darkness and no longer wants to lie quietly. He mutters a bit, plays with his fingers and toes, laughs. Behind the wall, in the living room, are soldiers. They are searching, rummaging, pounding on the wall! They open the buffet! They laugh. They found the vodka. They drink it, shout, laugh. And it seems to be going on forever! As long as the child does not cry. The mother holds it close to herself, closing his mouth using hers.

Finally the villains gather and leave. So the second day passed. Only to hold out one more day!

The third, final day. Again soldiers flood the apartment. Today they are especially vicious, noisy. Just like mad dogs, they growl at every corner. Their steps can now be heard. But today the child is unbearably whimsical. Is he sick? As long as he does not cry. He is crying! Now they are climbing he stairs. Again they enter the apartment.. One of the neighbors throws a pillow on the child. The mother wants to shout at him. But it is all in vain, the villains heard them. They push the buffet over and enter the room.

All of those in the room were taken to Ponary.

Gens again assures us that all will be calm. He convenes an assembly and announces that as though the Germans have assured him that now, since only the best and required artisans remain in the ghetto, nothing bad will occur again. It is only necessary for them to work hard and diligently, to be obedient. If we will provide a benefit with our effort and will be zealous in observing all the orders, they will not shoot us.

I saw myself how one person, after hearing these words, waved his hand and spit and called Gens a German scarecrow.

At this assembly Gens announced a new protocol: a responsible brigadier will be assigned to each brigade, a *kolonnenführer*.[55] He will answer for the entire brigade and must watch, while people are leaving for work, in case someone else attaches himself to that brigade and so attempts to enter the city. The brigadier will answer for orderly conduct when they walk through the city streets. He is responsible to have a list of the workers in his brigade and verify that they all arrived at work, and then demand a note from the doctor if they did not. Regarding those not working without a reasonable excuse he is responsible to report them to the ghetto *Arbeitsamt*. Then the police authorities will place this "saboteur" in prison for the night, while in the morning he will be released under the condition that he go directly to work.

"Among other things the work is compensated. Men will each receive one mark and 20 pfennings per day, women each —

---

[55] Column leader or gang leader

one mark, while each teenager up to the age of 16 years – 80 pfennings. This is what will be paid the worker. The employer will also be required to pay the same amount to the *Gebietskommissar*.

"But let no one think that this meager earning will go directly to the worker. No. He has the responsibility to support the ghetto authorities. This will consist of 10% tax. Then there are other special taxes to be paid. If these taxes are not paid, then food ration cards will not be distributed.

"Then another 10% for the committee for winter assistance. There is nothing you can do about this. The closer the winter, the more this subsidy is needed."

The remaining workers at *Kailis* already left the ghetto. Their director got his second house for allowing the new location for workers. Sad that we were not able to leave with them. So far it is calm there. During the time of the previous *aktions*, when blood was spilled all over this place and almost 7,000 persons were herded to Ponary, only a superficial inspection occurred there.

Now in our ghetto additional barriers will be installed. All those who work at the same place must live at the same place, be together. People say that this is a bad sign. Now if someone is laid off, immediately he will be taken to Ponary. No way can he hide. Another person is relieved, that maybe all of this is a display of typical German pedantry, their love for detail, or in the worst case, a new means of catching people who do not have yellow identification cards.

If this is genuinely the only reason they are doing this, then it is in vain. Those who do not have identification cards stayed where they are. The apartments were now more crowded but we managed to live. As far as the "illegals" are concerned, no one seems to know anything about them, not the German officers, not the ghetto police.

More gloomy news. The families of Soviet officers were taken to Ponary. Up to this time they were held in two houses at Subachayus Street. A song was passed along to us, composed by a 13-year old boy confined at Ponary:

> Two houses stand on Subach Street
> Two houses that were Jewish,
> Now Soviet people sit,
> The Jews were killed at Ponary.[56]

Today they were taken away. One woman while driving by shouted at the brigade returning to the ghetto, "Where is the worker's village of Ponary? They are taking us there to work."

The typical deception...

An order was issued by the *Gebietskommissar*. "Jews are prohibited to birth children. The nation doomed to annihilation must not birth a new generation."

Today they prohibit us from having babies, but tomorrow they can kill those that are already here.

Can't I just live one day without having to face the fear of death.

The previous night an additional *aktion* occurred. It was clandestine, and an unusually quiet one, so we did not hear about it until today.

On this occasion death penetrated a family of workers at a factory that is under the administration of the Gestapo. Although working in the very belly of the beast is more terrifying, but it did have one advantage: The brigadier was able to acquire a grant to include all the members of the family in the new identification cards, meaning, not only wife and children, but also parents, sisters and brothers. Of course attempting to save as many people as possible they each

---

[56] The verse rhymes in Russian.

inherited a large number of relatives. But now the authorities caught up with them. They had far too many employed and the number of family members was even greater.

About midnight a small group of soldiers stealthily entered the ghetto and went straight to the blocks where the workers at the Gestapo shops lived (Strashuno Building 3 and half of 15). They quietly wakened the residents and related to them an order from chief Gestapo officer Noigeboer, for them to leave the ghetto. Their polite and normal tone of voice had them think that they came to have them bring some workers out of the ghetto, and who apparently were in some kind of danger.

Some unrelated families also lived on these blocks, and who were tardy in moving to their new block. Now they considered themselves fortunate and joined the others who were leaving.

All were taken to the Lukiskes prison. But this did not scare them. During the period of the first *aktion*, against those without yellow identification cards, when it was necessary for them to stay with their families for a day where they worked, they were instead held overnight at one of the local jails.

In the morning the prison supervisor, Vais, entered their cell with several Gestapo police and announced that the majority of workers were now laid off from work. He would read the names of those whom he needed from a list and they would return to the ghetto. But now their previous privileges not longer applied, only their wives and children under the age of 16 could leave. Parents and other relatives and all the others laid off would remain there.

The released were only a handful and they returned to the ghetto.

The remaining no doubt were taken to Ponary.

Again disorder. Those who possess yellow identification cards are required to fill out questionnaires. Mama already completed hers. The questions are regular: family name proper name, year of birth, vocation, place of employment, names of the members of the family, genders and their ages. Only those who had a blue ticket filled out the questionnaires. They said that the members of the family that are noted in the questionnaires will be given pink identification cards.

So will they give it to every member or again do they plan on something else?

They will assign the pink identification cards to all, but not immediately. Only a certain quantity of people will received them each day.

Mama already received a set for us. Now I also have my personal document. Of course it is not so important, since it is applicable only in the ghetto and only Gens has his signature on it. Even the imprint indicates it is local: a six-pointed star with a subscription in German, "Police commander. Ghetto. Vilnius."

People have calmed. Once the pink identification cards were distributed to all of them in order, there was no more reason to worry.

But yesterday evening panic unexpectedly ensued. Murer wanted to finish this assignment before the next morning.

A regiment of soldiers entered the ghetto early in the morning. They arranged themselves in the streets. Of course they are waiting until all the workers leave for the city. But people do not want to leave. Gens with his police force is threatening to use force. He makes the announcement that his intent is only to make a verification: if they find anybody with a yellow identification card who has not left for work, they will annul the card and arrest them and the entire family.

Nonetheless mama does not want to go. The neighbors practically had to force her to go.

What will happen to us? Maybe at least this time they will not fool us and they will actually just verify our identification. It is still a bad situation. The neighbors residing in our apartment do not have identification cards. They registered their child with a friend, while during the previous two *aktions* they survived at the shelter of a friend's residence. They temporarily destroyed the existing shelter with the intent of wanting to make improvements on it. They have nowhere to go, so they decided to just hide in bed. They lay down and we covered them with blankets and pillows, all those we had in the apartment, and scattered our clothes on top.

It is a quiet winter morning. Rare snowflakes are circulating in the air. They create this transparent cover when they lie on the ground. But then leather boots trample them into the mud. Again another layer of snowflakes descending settles on them, as though wanting on their own to cover the mud and the impressions made by the boots. But the effort is futile. Now many feet are trampling them as they lead away a large group of people. Having survived two such horrifying *aktions*, they will nonetheless perish. It is difficult to escape Ponary.

Suddenly we hear footsteps. The soldiers are already in the yard! They are walking up the stairs! They are knocking on the apartment next door. No one is opening, they are breaking the door. She is shaking, a woman's cry. A soldier's laugh. Footsteps. Stomping. They are leading someone out.

They are now knocking at our door! We throw them into bed, cover them, smooth it. Totally scared I sit on the bed. They are moving underneath me, obviously I am causing pain with my pressure.

The German officers are verifying every identification card. They are beating on the walls, they move the cupboard over, they growl walking through the living room. The rush into the next room. I carefully pick up he corner of the pillow so to allow a little air to penetrate for the suffocating souls.

The villains are leaving. We throw off the pillows. We dust them off and give them some cold water. The people are finally able to catch their breath. But they decide not to get out of bed just in case the Gestapo return.

There are covered trucks standing at the gates to the ghetto. On this occasion the executioners were not herding their sacrifices on foot, because the tendency was for them to attempt to escape, even though a bullet will more than likely catch up with any daredevil. So if they take them by truck less worry for an attempted escape.

They will take them to a forest. For a long while the sound of gunshots. Then it will again become quiet. And only the trees, as if petrified in mourning, will honor the memory of the executed.

The neighbor also received a pink identification card. After the distribution to the members of the family some blanks were available. Workers are needed and so they gave the pink cards to all who were able to survive the recent horrifying *aktions*.

This means that they will no more impose on them. This is how Aunt Rosa was incorrect, who immediately lost hope. She could have hid, perhaps, and lived in the manner that we are living. True, but for how long? In any case, we who are still alive have the capacity to hope, but her?

The neighbor has the same type of identification card as we do, except next the number there is the letter S, that he is not a direct member of the family, but under their shelter – *schutz*. His vocation is also recorded there. The neighbor's wife has a regular identification card as a member of the family, just like the rest of us.

So now they have ordered to work not just those who received these cards, but in general all the residents of the ghetto: women, old people, teenagers. Those who work will also get a blue identification card, which verifies that they are working, in addition to the pink.

I also want to work in the city, but mama does not allow me. She says I will freeze, and so now is she supposed to leave the youngsters by themselves? But I feel that soon she will give in, because there is very little income between her and Miriam.

Nevertheless this would add some more money to our income, but most important, and perhaps, I will also be able to bring something here from the city.

Hurray! The fascists are being resisted! They are being pushed back from Moscow! The Red Army has already liberated Kalinin.[57]

Bad for them as they will now freeze!

What is pathetic is that they want to dress warmer at our expense. We were ordered to give up all of our overcoats, even scarves, fur hats and vests. All clothing made of fur must absolutely be brought to the *Judenrat* before 5 o'clock. If the order is not fulfilled the penalty is capital punishment. If this is not enough to spite us, the cold is terrifying, no one remembers such a severe winter. But the occupiers do not need to deal with it, as they enter the ghetto each day, recruit women and even teenagers, and haul them off to shovel snow. The work is temporary, and so they are not given any identification cards, and not even any earned income. They plainly haul them away and force them to work.

We have no choice but to deliver. But the majority of people work in the street. The only people who froze up to this time are those who felt the war would end before winter, and so did not bring to the ghetto their winter jackets, but now for sure everyone will freeze.

Mama gathered our scarves and took them. She said that at the *Judenrat* a truck is parked and into which they are loading complete armfuls of warm hats, scarves and jackets.

I ran to take a look. Yes. Loaded automobiles were driving out of the ghetto. And in their place empty ones arrive to quickly leave from here, slowly hauling baskets piled with differently colored fur remnants.

---

[57] The name of the city Tver, between 1931 and 1990. Liberation on December 5, 1941.

Today I heard an anecdote: The Red Army thought that they took captive a women's battalion, since the German soldiers' overcoats had silver fox tails hanging out of them.

How could we have survived without the teacher Jonaitis? No doubt we would be malnourished worse. Last week he brought us a clay pot filled with fat. His mother brought it to him from the countryside, included a greeting card with it, but he did not noticed the card, meaning he did not open the package. As soon as he received it he brought it directly to us. He is very careful, yesterday he brought my father's autumn coat to the ghetto gates and gave it to Miriam, while he is himself walking about in torn boots. Mama already asked him several times to wear papa's boots that he left at his house. In the final end he promised, but under the conditions that mama take money for them.

What else?

It has been quiet for several days. I will attempt to describe our life in more detail.

People here all live differently. Some who arrived at the ghetto brought with them large items; others have friends in the city that provide assistance; a third group has neither one nor the other. Occasionally the Department of Social Services under the administration of the *Judenrat* will provide some help. They will provide the means to pay the rent for the apartment (if it is not paid, you do not receive ration cards), they will intervene for privileges when taxes are paid, they will give passes for the bathhouse or coupons for soup for free. Of course to receive any of these is not easy, there are more needy than there are opportunities.

Recently the Social Services and Winter Assistance brought a collection of clothes, and summoned people. The intent was to distribute them beginning with those who had the least or nothing, and the people all shared it among themselves.

These clothes went first to orphans and those walking in tatters, those who shoveled snow in the city streets, and who worked on the railway and at the airport.

Among other things, to work at the airport is a genuine misfortune. The German soldiers there are terrible, and their greatest pleasure is to aim a gun at someone's hat or to after work force the exhausted and frozen people to crawl on their stomachs across the runway until late at night.

Another *aktion* occurred. Not a large one, it was quiet, but nonetheless an *aktion*.

A small regiment of soldiers quietly entered the ghetto at night. Stealthily and calmly they ordered the ghetto police to remain in their positions, while they departed to addresses on their list.

They awakened people rather politely, advised them to take with them warm clothing, and they patiently waited until they dressed and gathered their things.

It was only outside the ghetto gates, when they started to herd them into cars, that the people came to the realization of their predicament...

It seems that the night before Murer demanded new sacrifices from Gens. Gens created a list of ghetto police whom he now felt were undesirable or with whom he was fed up, and gave the executioners the addresses, and that night gunshots again rattled at Ponary.

I did not know that illegal organizations of communists and *komsomols* were active in the ghetto. No one released their names, otherwise this could cause them harm. But the fact is, they did exist. The best proof was the New Year's summons.[58] Genuine, printed (and maybe even in the ghetto?). The notices fervently summoned resistance, meaning, not to allow themselves to be massacred like helpless sheep. They wrote

---

[58] January 1, 1942

81

already that at Ponary our mothers, brothers and sister lie. Enough sacrifices! We need to go to war!

This raised our mood. Everyone was repeating the words of the summons.

So did the New Year of 1942 begin. The people however did not congratulate one another in the regular tradition, because this year was liable to be our last year. They talked that Hitler in his new year address on the radio announced that by the eve of the year, meaning the 1943 New Year, you will have to go to a museum to see a Jew and he will look like a scarecrow.

If Hitler does not die on the front, he is liable to materialize his threats.

Our neighbor spent last night at the ghetto jail. They caught him attempting to bring some potatoes into the ghetto.

This jail is located at building 6, Strashuno St, in the same yard as the library. Factually this is Lidskaya St, since from this side it is walled so nothing can be heard from the other side, and the entrance is through the yard from Strashuno St.

The jail has several cells. Petty criminals are confined there, those sentence for not going to work, attempting to bring something into the ghetto or for insulting the ghetto police. These cells are always packed full.

Initially people would laugh at this jail, but now they fear the place. It is often serves as a transfer point before going to Ponary. When Murer needs people to shoot, the first thing Gens does is clean out the jail.

I will now describe our government organization.

The organization we have is much like the local government. As over there are ministries, departments and committees, while here is the *Judenrat* and its departments and police.

Other than the *Arbeitsamt*, the Department of Social Services, the library and hospital, of which I already wrote, there are many others.

The department of food distribution distributes ration cards through the commanders of the residences, he decides what and how much food needs to be in the grocery stores and controls their distribution.

The department over the apartments deals with the question of rooms, specifically the corners in rooms. If after an *aktion* some room now has more space, people are transferred there, those living in a worse confined condition, and in a previously decided order. The department of apartments maintains a repair brigade that occasionally will paint the rooms. But sadly this fortunate opportunity only affects the members of the police and other privileged groups.

The ghetto also has other organizations: the mechanical and financial departments, the workshop department, the registration bureau, and even a funeral service. There is nothing you can do in this case, people do die from reasons other than due to a bullet. The city authority has assigned for the ghetto's use a covered black hearse and a retired horse to pull it. Almost every morning at dawn in the ghetto a crowd of mourners have a funeral procession – a black hearse and a handful to accompany it. If they have two or three coffins at the same time to bring out the procession is larger.

But they only get as far as the ghetto gates and the relatives there bid them farewell.

One person softly weeps, another cries. The gates open and swallow the hearse and again close. The next minute the clatter of hoof steps is heard against the sleeping pavement, and that is all... Now they rush the deceased through the streets to the cemetery. They need to hurry before the city wakens, even for a dead *Jude* not all the services can be provided.

The children are handled by a special department of supervision. For orphans there are boarding schools. The children are divided into groups, by age. The younger attend school in the morning while later work in ghetto workshops or at special brigades where they transport stuff. The younger teenager, even if an orphan, works in the city, they do not accept him at a boarding school. They count him as already being an independent person, even though in reality he is not very old.

There are two schools, on Strashuno and Shyaulu Streets. They were especially located further from the gates. If a German officer of some sort unexpectedly glances inside the ghetto he does not need to know how many children are here, he does not need to see that they are being cared for. The teachers themselves drug tables and school desks there, and even found some chalkboards. They teach, and without textbooks. Chemistry without laboratory exercises, biology without one plant, but they teach.

Every day at 12 o'clock noon the children are led into the kitchen for soup. They walk hitting the floor with their cloth-lined wooden shoes, and they wait to be allowed in. They have been dreaming about this minute the entirety of the night before and all of the morning.

Greedily they swallow their portion, licking the bowl. They leave and again start to wait for tomorrow when they will again be brought here.

Children. Pale faces with soiled wooden shoes over their feet. They are also the enemies of the *fuehrer*. He also feels he needs to cleanse Europe of them.

There is a high school for the older teens, but it is half-empty. Not because there are less people of this age group, but because they are already working. They do not consider themselves, nor do others consider them anymore, as children.

I guess I forget that I just turned 15 years of age.[59] Better for me not to think about it, because the desire to want to learn and read verses overwhelms me and I want to sob! Now I would love to learn theorems and even physics. But mama and Miriam are working, I need to watch over the children, take my turn.

It is not at all good to envy, but sometimes I envy the youngsters who do not understand anything. In the dirty narrow yard, under gloomy oppressive roofs they dance and sing. Their little eyes shine.

A few days ago in the morning an announcement appeared stating that the second police regiment together with some artists is preparing a presentation. Along with this announcement another opposing one quickly appeared, "They do not allow singing at the cemetery! The police regiment is content with their life, they are fed and clothed, and now they want to arrange concerts. People! Do not attend the concerts. Instead of sitting at some concerts, it is better to think of ways to harm the Germans."

But the concert was performed although very few spectators attended.[60] Now the department of culture of the *Judenrat* wants to start a theater.

Last night they bombed. For us a festive day.

We were already laying in bed when suddenly the windows shook from a horrible explosion. We jumped in fright, thinking that they are bombing the ghetto. Another explosion. Someone cried, "Bombs!"

Hurray! They are liberating us! But mama assures us that one bombing raid will not change anything. So that means we will get more bombs! No one will feel sorry for them for doing this!

---

[59] She jumps here in her diary as she will turn 15 on July 21, 1942.
[60] January 18, 1942

Gens and his police regiments are total insane. If they notice even the light of a cigarette in some window they will throw a rock at it. Bombs are exploding, glass is falling, police are whistling, to them it is the end of the world. But it is not frightening for me. On the contrary.

Suddenly the sounds fade. The planes have flown away and again we are by ourselves, in the laps of the enemy.

The planes have returned a second time, somewhere in the distance the silence is being interrupted, and then a prolonged quietness right after. It seems one bomb fell not far from the ghetto.

About noon a raging Noigeboer rushes in. Someone told him that white flares were released from the ghetto during the night. This means that people here knew about the airplane attack and were waiting for them. The Jews illuminated the city for the Bolsheviks, to allow the planes to get better oriented. It was no use to try and find the guilty. For such treachery everyone had to answer. [Noigeboer] personally and with his own hands will incinerate the ghetto, "With their burning bodies these Jews can illuminate their friends the communists."

I have not recorded anything for a long while. Life is monotonous. If we are not talking about Ponary, then we complain about not enough to eat. Several times I saw A.R. But what can I talk to him about? About school? How long can a person retain memories? There is nothing else about which to speak. He works, I have my own responsibilities. I can talk to mama about them if I need to talk to somebody, but not with him.

It is already March. It will soon be spring.

Our life is again worrisome: the term of the validity of yellow identification cards is expiring.

In autumn when we received these cards, five months for their validity seemed like a long term. March 30, seemed so far away. We could at least live this much longer! We hoped that by this day the German occupation would be forced out. Now this day is approaching, and they are still here.

Every person who has any imagination is trying to figure out what will next happen to us. However nothing is heard. I guess no Gestapo policeman or someone serving in the *Gebietskommissar* has said anything to anyone. The secrecy causes a suspicion of only something bad.

Now I know exactly. There are illegal organizations active in the ghetto and which are ready to enter into open struggle against the occupiers. This is the FPO – The United Partisan Organization. The members of this organization have already manufactured with their own hands a mine and which they have placed under the railway near Naujoji Vilnia.[61]

Hurrah!

However we could not talk about this. Mama even prohibited me from recording it in my diary. But how can I dismiss such news?

The men of our apartment were on rotating guard the final three nights before the expiration of the validity of the yellow identification cards. If an *aktion* was to occur, at least it would not catch them unaware of it.

Today is the last night, no one is going to bed.

It is almost a spring night, but it is getting cold and motionless in some kind of way, it seems to be getting darker and darker.

Finally light from the dawn. We walk outside to the street. Do we need to go to work, or not? The ghetto police, of course,

---

[61] or, New Vilna, a neighborhood in eastern Vilnius, through which the Warsaw-Petersburg train passes, and eventually a suburb was built around it.

are making an announcement for us not to panic and go to work as we always do. But someone started a rumor that the Gestapo will transfer to Ponary those who leave and right from work, while the ghetto will be "cleansed" during the day.

The brigades scattered. Everyone is running home to hide, to save themselves, to resist. The ghetto police are catching them and forcing them to go to work.

And mama was almost coercively led away. I hid in the yard so I would not have to bid farewell to her.

The day passed in intensive expectation. But nothing happened. It is already night?

Dressed we tried to sleep. The night likewise passed calmly. Perhaps the Germans just forgot that the term had expired?

They extended the identification cards. But not everyone was issued one immediately to avoid a panic.

Mama's was extended. They plainly scribbled over the date of March, 30, 1942, and place a stamp: April 30. Just for one month. The optimists assure us that during this interval they will print new work permits and which they will distribute in place of the yellow cards.

On this occasion the rumors will correct. The yellow cards were eventually replaced by work permits. I already saw one. They are made of sturdy pink paper. On the first page, meaning the cover, is a place for family name, proper name, date and place of birth, place of residency (but here the space is already printed with: Vilna. Ghetto), vocation and gender and marital status. The next two pages are reserved for information from their place of employment: where and what, when hired, when terminated. At the end of the permit is a place for authorization by the ghetto authorities.

When all those who presently have a yellow card get a work permit, they will then distribute an additional blue card to the same people.

Among other things, the appellation of blue card is not entirely precise, as right now they are printed on green and white paper, obviously because they ran out of blue.

Mama and I already long agreed that once spring arrived I will also go to work. And so now I work. I haul water.

The first morning, leaving the ghetto, I got scared: there were so many German soldiers in the street! I drug myself together with the balance of the brigade and was afraid to lift my eyes. And the streets were so wide and clean. Here it was brighter than in the ghetto.

I saw my French language teacher, Bakaitis. Maybe I should not have gotten his attention, then he would not have nodded back. Maybe this would back fire on him if someone notices.

I work in the vegetable gardens of an aged rich man, Palevich. His home is rather far, and specifically in the region of the Kalvariski marketplace. The boss is a mean person. The first day I was there he warned us not to dare steal even one carrot from there. If we should eat one carrot or cucumber while weeding he will forgive us, but if he should catch us attempting to take them with us he will relate this to the Gestapo.

For the meanwhile there is nothing to weed or eat. We carry water for watering. The initial buckets were extremely heavy for us, and even harder due to the distance we had to carry them, and to the ends of the garden-beds. This distance was two blocks relative to the ghetto.

I carried full buckets and hurried back with the empty ones. Time just dragged. When it was time for lunch, the Polish women who were working there not far from us sat to eat. As much as I wanted to take a look at what they were eating, I forced myself to turn away, or else they will think that I am begging them for food. Of course, if they would have offered me some, I would not have turned away.

After sitting for a while it was hard to stand. My entire body was hurting. My hands were shaking from the strain and now the buckets seemed heavier. I had a hard time getting back to work.

The sun set very slowly.

That evening mama could not convince me to eat: I vomited, my head hurt. Mama says that I was intoxicated due to having so much fresh air. But why I was sick was not important to me.

I could not get out of bed in the morning. Mama begged, explaining that if I am working I cannot skip even one day, otherwise I will be labeled a saboteur. She helped me get dressed as though I was a child, but I complained of how bad I was treated, that she – mama – did not understand me, she just could not imagine how hard it was for me. But mama dressed me and calmed me saying that this is always how it is at the first day of heavy work and then it goes away.

Yesterday it indeed was easier, and today rather tolerable.

So work would not become monotonous, and for the time to pass faster, I count the buckets. Today I hauled 96. I brought two full buckets on each of 48 trips.

The Soviet Union made an alliance with England and America. They decided that they will together war against Hitler and his confederates.

Information about the alliance between the three governments was precise, and all the information about what as occurring at the front was reliable. Those communists acting illegally in the ghetto were distributing among the populace information that they acquired from the *Sovinformburo*.[62]

For a long while no new directives were implemented, and then suddenly the *burgomaster*[63] ordered that every resident of the ghetto pay a personal tax for the second half of this year.

---

[62] Soviet Information Bureau
[63] similar to a mayor of a city, in this case the ghetto

My share of the personal tax was eight marks. This would not be so expensive if I had the money, but I did not. And there was almost nothing left to sell. The children seemed to understand this. A few days ago a neighbor asked Ruvik what he eats. Not thinking he answered, "The sleeve of my mama's nightgown."

We are fortunate that such a person as Jonaitis is in the world.

It has been a year since the occupation started. How has life changed, so many people have perished! How this years is so unlike all the previous years. Right now in the ghetto, if there are no *aktions,* every day is the same as the previous.

Early morning. Sleepy people are entering Rudninka St, they collect into brigades. Children with wooden trays hanging from their necks wander between them advertising their wares, "Saccharin! Cigarettes! Who wants cigarettes? Flint for lighters!" Women quietly offer flatbread made from rye flour.

A few chimney sweeps are returning from the city. These are the most wealthy people of the ghetto. While children the chimney sweeps were afraid that they would remain dirty once becoming adults, as they were always covered with soot, but now others envy them as they are always well fed. The matter is that there are not enough chimney sweeps in the city, and so the city administration was compelled to turn to the Gestapo for them to allow them to get chimney sweeps from the ghetto, and especially to grant them the guarantee that they have this right to walk through the city unaccompanied and enter homes. There was written on the back side of the chimney sweep's identification card, that this *Jude* could alone, without supervision, walk along the streets. After finishing cleaning the chimney benevolent people would often feed them and sometimes give them something for their family. The guards at the ghetto entrance would avoid checking their grimy toolboxes. They never fell into Murer's hands. The chimney sweeps would work early in the morning and were already returning at about the time that other workers were getting ready to leave.

Little by little the ghetto empties, the brigades leave for work. Individual pedestrians appear in the streets. These persons work for the *Judenrat*. They wear cleaner clothes, but appear very pale, as if fragile.

The motorized saws start to operate. The ghetto as if again becomes alive, every the hum of electrical saws are heard.

The tired workers return in the evening.

Night set in. All freezes until the next morning.

When I returned home from work today it was still quiet at the gates.[64] Suddenly an alarm occurred. I look. The ghetto police are herding from behind the barrier those they are encountering and stopping movement. Murer is at the gates! He is standing at the entrance and observing how the police who are responsible for guarding the gates are searching those entering. Occasionally he will search someone himself. They found one woman who had 20 pfennings on her (only 10 pfennings are permitted). He orders her to be taken to the building that serves as a sentry post, unclothe her and punish her with 25 lashes with sticks. Five policeman beat her, each of them five times. But for Murer this is not enough so he takes a stick and continues himself.

Leaving the half-living woman behind Murer returns to the gates. The scene of them beating her irritated him and he now seeks new sacrifices.

He notices that one aged man has something that is sticking out from under his jacket. It is a kettle of soup. Murer orders him to immediately eat right there all of the soup. Since he feels he does not get enough from his ration cards, let him eat his fill. The person starts to eat. But it is hard for him to do this. A sympathetic well-doer already fed him and this soup

---

[64] June 15, 1942

was designated for his family. But he could not explain this to Murer. He laughs at him, vexes him. If he will not eat it and lick it clean he will go to Ponary. The man swallows, forcing it down.

In the end Murer is tired of fooling with the man. He hollers at him, "To the left." His assistants take the criminal and haul him to the prison. People die just because they wanted to bring a crust of bread home to their children.

There is still no second front[65] and it is apparent the German troops are hurrying to take advantage of this, continuing to advance. A bloody battle for the Crimea. Sebastopol is being heroically defended.

The ghetto is not happy. The heat is intense. It is difficult to work. I don't even want to eat. But a soon liberation is still not apparent. Of course the ground under the occupiers' feet burn. Regiments of partisans are being created. I heard that our ghetto is also being armed. In short, people are motivated. But all is occurring very clandestinely.

Again another panic. Several carts drove up to the gates. Two soldiers sat in each of them. Their officer entered the ghetto and asked for Gens to deliver them elderly and weakened people to "take to a summer home for rest."[66]

There are few elderly in the ghetto. It is very difficult to survive under such conditions. But there are some new arrivals here who somehow prematurely aged. Some live with their families, others live alone, in a shelter. The shelter is a group of several dark and smelly rooms with beds packed together. The very weak aged do not even get up, and those who do walk appear more like shadows than like people.

---

[65] She is referring to the USA and Great Britain planned invasion which had not yet started.

[66] July 17, 1942

And so by Gens' order the ghetto police started to assemble all the aged people, repeating to them like parrots the words of the German officers, that there is nothing to fear. They are being taken to Pospeshke[67] to a summer home. But who believes them?

They started of course with the shelter to take those who were not in any condition to get up on their own. The carts entered the ghetto. The police carried the helpless skeletons and piled them on the carts.

Others were brought right from their homes. The *aktion* started so suddenly that no one succeeded in hiding.

The German soldiers attempted to display themselves courteously, not laughing, not shouting. They even ordered the aged to be accompanied by a nurse and some police officers. They figured the carts would soon return to get the cook, their bread ration for the day, kettles and other kitchen utensils.

What did this mean?

Those police who accompanied the aged assured them that they actually just returned from Pospeshke, and where all was prepared for their rest. Of course they were lying.

So what was supposed to change? The aged here rested plenty. They were fed decently, were not beaten, their photographs were taken. So all of their relatives remaining in the ghetto begged Gens to return the aged. But he did not want to hear them, affirming to them that nothing threatens the aged, and after a two-week period of rest they will return to the ghetto.

Of course, they just invented all of this.

This morning the German officers again demanded from Gens his policemen; they needed to return the aged to the ghetto. For some technological reasons they could not hold as many of them there that they wanted.

---

[67] a suburb of Vilnius

The policemen left, all sat in some cars and they left for the city, but they never returned to the ghetto.

The more we thought about it the more clear it was where all of them were being taken.

This time it was the ghetto police who were agitated, as they were accompanied to the place of death. I guess murderers do not like living witnesses to their crimes.

But some returned. Just some. So more than a 100 grey haired aged collapsed into the pit.

So why was this tragic-comedy of a so-called "rest retreat" needed? That we could not figure. But in every case it is clear the fascists wanted to flex their muscle to them.

Soon it will be autumn. The occupiers decided to reserve fuel. To hew trees in the forest, of course, they need people from the ghetto. It seems strange that they are promising to give half the hewn wood to the ghetto. I guess they are afraid that our residents will not be very concerned about their warmth. This way maybe they will interest us. The more wood chopped, the more the ghetto will get.

Gens announced that all those men who are not working must immediately, at that very moment, register at the *Arbeitsamt*. But they do not believe that they will be taken someplace to work, they are scared and so searching for some means of escaping it. But no one is helping. They said that those working at the privileged *Judenrat* will then have to work in the forest an assigned number of days. And good, let them feel what physical labor is like.

But the German officers are postponing sending anyone. They say it is because the forests are full of partisans who are blowing up bridges, or causing the trains to derail. The German officers are afraid that people from the ghetto will join the partisans.

Nonetheless the Germans are still driving people from the ghetto to the forest. Of course they ordered Gens to send the ghetto police with them, and who will supervise them, so the wood-choppers will not escape and join the partisans. If this does happen then it will be *kaput* for the entire ghetto.

Yesterday the ghetto police worked until late in the evening distributing a summons to each person assigned to work in the forest.

Panic arose. People running to hide. But the ghetto police are catching them and forcing them. They repeat Gens' words that there is nothing to fear, that they are definitely being taken to the forest to work, otherwise why would the ghetto police also be sent with them and even the *dienstleiter*.[68] However this argument did not calm anybody. The German officers would not spare a few ghetto police in their desire to deceive us.

Someone started a rumor that they are not driving us to chop trees, but to clear the fields of mines.

Those gathering at the *Arbeitsamt* look more like grave diggers than like wood-choppers. Some took with them some kinds of packages, while others came with nothing in their hands. In any case, why take clothes with you, better to leave it home for the family, at least they could sell it.

It is noon. The first of 10 wagons are leaving the ghetto. Each one has a German officer on it. The women are loudly sobbing, the ghetto police are chasing them away. The gates are opened and then they are closed, the people depart into obscurity.

Those taken are definitely working in the forest. Some women received letters from their husbands. Some peasant in the city shoved them into a brigade that was passing.

All ran joyously to read these letters.

---

[68] Service Leader, a high ranking Nazi party member

Getta, with whom I work at the vegetable garden, has long been trying to convince me to join the choir. She says it is very interesting, but especially because it will allow me to forget about our misfortunes for a while.

A few days ago she took me there. The choir director, Durmashkin,[69] tested my voice, hearing, memory and ordered me to immediately remain for an audition. But the choir it seems sings in the old Hebrew language, of which I understand nothing.

The members of the choir explained that it will initially be hard for me. It seems that after each *aktion* they lose some members. So now they need to attract more to join. But this is not easy: Some explain that they tire easily, for others their parents do not allow them, others are in mourning. Other than this, often after an *aktion*, rocks were thrown at the windows so they would not sing. The choir did not even have a place to practice, each time it gathered somewhere else. But nevertheless they managed to practice every Tuesday and Friday. Now the choir has two rooms on Strashuno St, Building 12, a piano and even a stage.

Among other things, Durmashkin's choir is not the only one. There is a choir under the supervision of Slep.[70] They sing in Hebrew there. This choir has a beautiful soloist, Luba Levitzkaya, who earlier sang on the radio.[71]

Durmashkin created a symphony orchestra. This of course was more difficult. Very few musicians survived. If a person proudly claimed to be a musician he was already long at Ponary, instead of figuring ahead of time that it would be best to claim yourself a cabinet maker, or window installer, or at least a cobbler. Other musicians suddenly acquired for

---

[69] Wolf Durmashkin, 1908-1944. After the liquidation of the Vilnius ghetto he was taken to Klooga concentration camp in Estonia, and executed.
[70] Abram Slep, 1884-1943. Died at Kivioli concentration camp, Estonia.
[71] A popular Lithuanian singer and opera performer, and music teacher. 1909-1943. She was eventually executed by the Germans at the Ponary forest in January 1943.

themselves a new vocation and aspired as hard as possible to master it and so they would not be terminated. As a result their fingers coarsened and would not do what they were supposed to do with their musical instrument. Other than this, after 12 hours of hard work it was difficult for them to hold a violin in their hands, much less even want to. And often the person who wanted to did not have an instrument. Having been herded into the ghetto they did not succeed in taking it with them, or else long exchanged it for food.

But apparently the more difficult something is, the greater the enthusiasm. Somehow the orchestra was assembled. Durmashkin acquired music scores from some kind people at the Philharmonic. Right now the orchestra is preparing for Beethoven's *Ninth Symphony* together with the choir. We noticed the text of the fourth part of the symphony is Schiller's *Ode to Joy*. We translated it into our own language.[72] There it makes a statement that all people are brethren. Of course, it is sad that the German soldiers do not consider this so.

Today could have been the last day of my life. But this morning I did not suspect anything, and so I went to work as usual. At midday I did not foresense anything. On the contrary I was rather in a good mood as I succeeded in trading mama's blouse for some flour.

Pouring the flour into a special quilted corset I waited for the evening when I would hang it under my dress and attach it with a rope so I would not look so fat, and so adjusting my posture I returned to the ghetto.

While we were walking from work, some passing person muttered to us not to walk any further, as there was some unrest near the ghetto.

We become puzzled. What was I to do? Where would I go? What was occurring in the ghetto? Maybe another *aktion*? The

---

[72] This would be Yiddish.

brigadier ordered us to proceed because our perplexity just might cause suspicion.

Barely, barely did we move forward. Some advised that we should return to work. Others were convinced that if we were to do so at night, to go in the opposite direction, this would be suicidal.

And then another passer-by warned us not to walk any further. They are doing intense searches at the gates.

This meant Murer. Those who were not carrying something were calmed. Others tried to discard unnoticeably while they were walking what they were hiding in their pockets, one potato at a time. But what was I to do with my bag of flour? I could not even remove it.

The ghetto was very close. I needed to do something to get their attention off of me, otherwise it will be too late. When they take me to Ponary I will fatally regret having to let this moment slip by.

Getta asked me to tear the star off her back, she will not enter the ghetto. I also will not go. I followed after her along the sidewalk. I was scared. Getta took me under her arm and we briskly walked. We just walked a short distance and it was already Kaunasskaya St. It is dangerous there, many pedestrians. We turned back. Through some alley we turned on Bolshaya Stefanovskaya St. But it was a short one and we were back on Kaunasskaya. We turn around to go back. We see the ghetto from a distance. There is still a regiment at the gates.

Again we make the same circular route, but how many times can we do this? If someone should notice they will quickly figure what we are doing. We crossed Kaunasskaya St and walked along unfamiliar streets.

It got dark. Very soon no doubt they will not be allowing individuals back into the ghetto. Maybe all the brigades have already returned and we will have no way to get in? We need to keep walking.

We kept ourselves at a distance but close enough to see
what was occurring at the gates, and there was still a rather
large crowd there, but by now they were calm. We started to
walk closer. We wanted to blend into a brigade passing by, but
they would not allow us, not wanting to put themselves at risk.
While we were explaining our situation we walked alongside
them, one foot on the sidewalk and the other on the pavement,
getting closer to the ghetto. Getta pulls me by the shirtsleeve,
we walk on the sidewalk, and somehow we were able to succeed
to walk past the ghetto.

Again we wander through the dark streets. The windows
are masked, we walk almost by touch. Going around in circles
we exited onto Pilimo Street. A crowd from a distance is coming
toward us along the pavement. No doubt one of our brigades.
Getta whispers to me that no matter how we do this we need to
get into the ghetto, otherwise we will risk remaining here the
entire night, and this means we will be arrested and taken to
the Lukiskes prison.

So as soon as the brigade got close enough to us we blended
into it. These people were more friendly than the other group.
A few treated us mean, grumbled, calling us – desperate girls,
but after listening to our explanation for our adventure, they
hid us in the center of themselves and promised to make us
less apparent to the ghetto police. One of them at the gates
actually put his hand on my shoulder to cover the area where
my star was supposed to me.

Murer was not at the gates any more. But the police worked
all the harder anyway and they did confiscate the flour that I
worked so hard to save, but no repercussions.

Mama had a had time dealing with my experience, "It is
good, Masha, that you are at least still alive." She thought I
was not going to return.

Only then did I discover what occurred. Just before evening
and right at when people were returning from word, Murer
unexpectedly drove up to the gates. He flew straight into the

street grocery store where confiscated goods were put on sale. Having seen what was little confiscated he flew back and beat several ghetto policemen. He shouted that they were not searching well enough.

A horrible panic arose in the ghetto. All were frightened, disoriented. Groups of violators were taken to the ghetto jail one after another. Women, seeing their husbands and brothers among the apprehended, sob, cry, curse. Murer's threats caused them all to get scared, saying that he will not tolerate those who ignore his orders. He forbid products to be brought inside the ghetto, while those *verdammte Juden* – accursed Jews – do not obey him. To give them all a lesson, 100 of the smugglers would be shot!

What then happened was that at night a portion of the apprehended were released from jail. Ten women were shot, those who worked at New Vilna and who fell directly into Murer's hands. They were hauled away. The convoy leader had to actually sign a paper that he received them from the warden of the ghetto prison and will answer for their safe transfer to Ponary.

Now it is November. Cold. Soon it will be winter. Will we endure the winter, even if no *aktions* occur?

One consolation is that this winter will for certain be the end for the German army. They are sorely being defeated. They have been besieging Stalingrad for such a long time but cannot succeed in taking the city. The Red Army is heroically defending each parcel of land, each building.

It is not just bad for the German army on the front, but also here in the occupied areas. One person told me in complete confidence that the ghetto partisans – the members of the FPO – are getting armed. The weapons of course are not being brought through the gates, but clandestinely smuggled using the most unusual of means: through the sewer pipes, under piles of wood, and even in coffins.

The same person told me that there are very few of these ghetto partisans, and Gens is responsible for this. He continually states that a person will only escape Ponary through observance of his orders and hard work. But if the authorities find out that there is even one partisan in the ghetto they will immediately demolish the entire ghetto.

The day before yesterday they brought the *dienstleiter* of the ghetto police to the ghetto, Shlossberg, who was seriously wounded in the stomach. Immediately after him Gens arrived at the hospital. There was no one with them while they were talking in the ward, so no one knows what the wounded was telling Gens. But they say that one of their own shot him. Shlossberg was threatening to expose Gens the entire time of having ties with the partisans who are active in the surrounding forests and that they are planning to join them. This is the reason his own wanted to get him out of the way.

Gens is now the official "sovereign" of the ghetto.[73] Up to this time everyone figured there were two officials: the president of the *Judenrat*, A.Freid, and the chief of the ghetto police, Ya. Gens (although up to this time Gens was de facto director [of the *Judenrat*]). Now it was officially announced that Gens has the authority and is fully authorized to direct the ghetto at his discretion. In short, he is now the *fuehrer* of the ghetto.

The chief of police will be Desler, who was formerly commander of the second ghetto. A.Fried was assigned as assistant to Gens in administrative affairs.

Getta told me much that was interesting about one *komsomol*, Sonya Madeisker. With a falsified passport, passing herself off as a Pole, she was able to pass through the frontlines

[73] Maria is inserting this into the diary out of chronological order. This event occurred on July 11, 1942.

and reach Veliki Luk. But they caught her. During interrogation she was silent. They threatened her with capital punishment. During her final night she succeeded in escaping from the fascists' clutches.

Sonya Madeisker then returned to Vilnius. She is living in the city illegally and, fearless of any dangers, continues to be active, helping to acquire weapons. She enters the ghetto and maintains connections with those communists working underground in the city.

Again bad news. Murer all of a sudden and for no reason started to inspect apartments.

The previous week he unexpectedly entered the ghetto and drove into the first courtyard that came to his mind. He kicked the first available door with his boot and rushed straight to the pantry for look at what product were there. After finding only a few loaves of bread he demanded to be shown what was cooking in the kettle. Once convinced that it was just water with some buckwheat he ran to the closet. He rummaged through it to try to find clothing without a star on it, but no such luck. Infuriated by his failure he entered the next apartment. Fortunately he also found nothing there that was prohibited.

A few days ago he again started his attacks. In one apartment he inadvertently noticed a tube of dried lipstick laying on the window sill that the residents overlooked. He beat up the woman who just happened to be there.

Immediately an order from Gens was posted on the streets (and I think this was the second of the type), where women are prohibited wearing decoration (interesting, if anybody still has any) or to use cosmetics.

Now the ghetto police must personally and diligently inspect the shelves, pots and cupboards in the apartments.

Up to this time hiding places were indispensable for people, but now they are needed for food.

My notes and verses I also hid. God have mercy on us should they be found, we will all be arrested. Mama says that I do not need to relate everything. She advises me to memorize what is most important, just in case they take my notebooks and destroy them., Mama is not about to put to risk the lives of the children and especially ourselves just for the sake of my recollections, if Murer will further search our apartment. This is why I decided to memorized as much of it that I could. I need to do this anyway, inscribe it on my mind and cram it into my head, as it is next to impossible to even find a scrap of paper while working at this cursed place.

The ghetto was expanded a little.[74] Several buildings on Mesino St up to Strashuno St were assigned to it. As a result the ghetto now reaches to Ashmenos St. Other than this they "gifted" us some parcels of several yards at different buildings, the rear end that is the border of the ghetto, but the building façade overlooks an unrestricted street, outside the ghetto limits, along Nemetzkaya St, these are buildings from 21 to 31. The entrance to these yards are through holes in the walls of the buildings along Mesino and Ashmenos Streets. Those whose apartments bordered the workshops or other necessary premises were relocated there.

We now live on Nemetzkaya St, Building 31. Our half of the yard is separated by an immensely high and thick wall. The bricks are solidly cemented together, there is not even the smallest crack through which we could possible see into the prohibited yard next door. Even the blank wall cuts through the balcony. What remains for us is a square of paved yard and a piece of the sky between the walls. It is as if we are retained inside a large four-sided dry well, out of which it is impossible to climb. The German officers inspected the area very meticulously so that the basements or attics of the adjoining

---

[74] September 8, 1942, again not in chronological order.

buildings also had barrier walls, and without the smallest opening remaining between them, even for a kitten.

A metal fabrication shop was brought into our yard. At Rudninka, Building 6, the table manufacturing shop was expanded, sewing and knitting shops were opened. Trucks would bring torn and blood-filled military jackets, gloves, socks and linen to the ghetto and they would leave with them clean, mended and patched.

The shoemaking shop was expanded, and especially the division making manila shoes. Here they would make women's shoes from manila or Davao hemp. They were different colors and very pretty. Touring German officials through the ghetto, Gens never avoided walking passed this division. There were always several dozen pairs of the prettiest shoes on display here as gifts. Bringing German officials here Gens would condescendingly politely consult with them, what pair the official seems to like most of all and where could he send them as a small souvenir from the ghetto. Gens would climb out of his hide to fawn the Gestapo officers. But this was not all.

There was also a chemical laboratory where shoe polish, toothpaste, facial powder, and even soap made from horse fat, was made. All of the products made here were taken into the city for the use of city officials.

There was even a clockmaker in the ghetto. Of course, not for us, but for the German officers. We almost already forgot what a clock even looks like. But the artisans were not interested in repairing our old ones, as it was not nearly as interesting as assembling new ones. One engineer with a group of specialists built an electric clock as a project for the ghetto as a surprise. And they hung it in the street at the corner of Rudninka and Disnos.

The clock had to be connected to the city grid, because the ghetto only received electric current a few hours each day.

It seems I forgot to mention that I no longer work at Palevich's, we were laid off. We are not needed during the winter.

I work at the barracks on Bolshaya St now. I need to clean the entire floor consisting of soldiers' bunks, the officers' rooms, the office, kitchen, corridor and stairs. Occasionally they also order me into the kitchen to peal potatoes.

The work is hard but it is profitable. Often the soldiers have some leftover soup. I pour it into a jar and then bandage my arm and tie a band to support it, while secure the jar of soup close to me with my elbow. If the ghetto policeman starts to search me at the gates, I give him the impression I am suffering due to the immense pain in my arm. Every time I do this I try to find a different policeman, otherwise he will notice it is the same arm all the time.

Three times I already brought a jar doing this.

Today I heard some terrible news. I did not yet tell mama about it.

At work, while we were peeling potatoes, the cook suffered an accidental violation of someone's lack of respect toward him. One of us, a female, did not approach him in the manner we were ordered. She did not call him by his title, "Respectable Gentleman Cook," but in some other manner, and so she was reprimanded. He then started to ask us where we were born, where we live, what we did before the war. I told him that previously lived in Plunge,[75] and when he heard this it made him happy. He served in the military with one man from Plunge – Benjamin Sheras, he was an electrician. On one Saturday, on the eve of the war, Benjamin was sent from the proving ground to Vilnius for some kind of wire. But then the war started and the Germans invaded. Discovering that he was a *komsomol*, they killed him and buried him in the yard just outside the barracks. The soldiers were too lazy to dig a deep

---

[75] City in north-west Lithuania, and near the Baltic Sea.

hole so they smashed him with rocks first and then covered him.

Benjamin was papa's first cousin.

Yesterday was a very worrisome day. For a long while mama did not return from work. We were getting ready to find someone from her brigade to find out what happened, but then she suddenly arrived. Apparently she removed her yellow stars and risked going to our old apartment in the city. She hoped she could find something from among our old stuff, as we had nothing remaining to sell or use to trade for food. She did not warn us ahead of time so we would not worry. It was all futile, as there was nothing there left to take.

She thought that we would not be able to endure a second winter here, yet we are still alive. There are some more hungry than us and wearing clothes that are completely tattered, but yet they are not as afraid as we are and do not feel as oppressed as we do. Of course we should not fear *aktions* any less, no, but now they are talking about matters other than this. Especially the men. They talk about the defeat of the German soldiers at the front, about the partisans in the forests, and the FPO in our ghetto.

I really like listening to these conversations. Then liberation seems to feel so much closer, almost tangible. I am starting to fantasize how all of this will occur, how we will be liberated, how we will return home, and encounter papa.

O, the sooner the better.

They shot the singer Luba Levitzkaya. So did Murer order. She died due to 1-1/2 kilograms of beans[76] that she wanted to bring into the ghetto.

Driving by, Murer saw Luba Levitzkaya and her friend Stupelia walking along Etmona Street. Murer stopped them and ordered them to show him what they were carrying. He

---

[76] About 4 lbs

found the beans on Levitzkaya and a potato on Stupelia. He gave an order to have them both taken to Lukiskes prison.

(That address will outlive us all.)

They said that Luba sang in prison. Even the soulless spectators did not prohibit her. She still had hope that they would save her. But days passed, her strength decreased, she started to whither and so did her hope. Levitzkaya did not suffer very long in prison, not quite two weeks. Assembling a group of criminals of this category the Germans took them all to Ponary.

They were driven there in a opened truck. Luba sang the entire route. As they were driving through the streets of the city the driver beat her up, for her to stop singing, but then he gave up: no act of violence was going to put her to silence and suddenly her crackling voice again started. She continued to sing! One song ended, another started, and so along the entire route. Even when she was in the pit she invoked her favorite song, *La Paloma*. But she was not able to finish it.

The German officials announced a period of mourning! For three days all the theaters, movies, restaurants and other entertainment businesses were to be closed.

Hurrah!!! They are sorrowful over their divisions that were defeated at Stalingrad. If we had someplace to organize a dance we would. This would be the first time since all of this started that I would dance! I would rejoice from all my heart. Finally the occupiers have to deal with a period of mourning.

And it is apparent that the Leningrad blockage has been broken![77] Now watch how they will be driven away, just watch how it will begin! But it is just February. They will all freeze!

I was relieved of my job at the barracks. Now I work at the *Vilnius* furniture factory as a polisher. From morning to

---

[77] January 18, 1943

evening I polish skis. There are not many to polish, but the skies need to shine. So I just wipe them all day long.

A few days ago they placed brochures on all the tables, workbenches and on the window sills. The occupiers are urging all the young people to relocate to Germany to work there. The brochures contain photographs of nice rooms with white beds and silk curtains. Under the pictures is an inscription that this is how all the arrivals will live. But none of the workers are in a hurry to register. The boss said that after these brochures were distributed, another one appeared the next day but clandestinely distributed. It said that the promises the Germans are making are all lies, a deception, and that the young people of Lithuania must not believe any of it. They need to remain here and fight against the oppressors to get their freedom.

The German troops are being forced out! Voronezh, Kharkov, Rostov, and many other cities are already liberated.

March. The first month of spring. But it does not feel this way here; it is still cold and dirty. And also melancholy, although some joy is felt in their local defeats. But then I think about this and realize that we are still so far away from the front. Even then each day can bring us some fatal disaster and so our hopes will be extinguished. No doubt a person needs to be very strong so to incessantly believe. Not only when there is good news from the front, but always, as right now, when they humiliate us, putting us on the same level as dogs, hanging numbered tags on our necks.

It was the Gestapo that no doubt decided we are not sufficiently labeled, that the stars and identification cards for such "dangerous elements" is not enough. They ordered the bureau of registration to introduce a re-registration – although based on previously provided data – and to issue "passports" and numbered tin tags.

The passport is a regular, yellow, study piece of paper folded in half. On it is our family name, personal name, middle name, year and place of birth, gender and marital status, color of eyes and hair, the form of our face and our height. There is also a place for fingerprints. But I was under the impression that fingerprints were only for criminals.

The numbered tag is round, made of plain tin. The edges are poorly trimmed. The tin tag has the six-cornered star impressed on it. At three of the corners are the letters VG (Vilnius ghetto), and W or M (female or male). At the top is a hole for a string.

Males and females register separately. And the number of the passport and other begin with the number One. There are several thousand more women than men.

We always need to carry on our person this document called a passport, while the numbered tag in general must never be removed from our neck – not daytime, not nighttime. The policemen who compose the guards at the gates are responsible to strictly verily that each person is wearing a numbered tag as they leave to work and when they return to the ghetto.

My skin became irritated the first day I had to wear this accursed tin plate. In addition to this it started to turn my skin black. Mama learned how to sew a small pocket from rags to hold it. We are also very resourceful in matters such as this one. But when this one German soldier noticed it he went wild. "Somehow or other those insolent *Judens* will protect their skin."

But what am I supposed to do if this tin rag causes me pain when it rubs against my skin? Someone else designed a new type of pocket: it is attached but open at the top. So if someone demands the tag to be shown, you pull it by the sting and it comes out, while the pocket stays on your stomach.

I just attended an interesting evening listening to rhythmic vinyl records. The little girls displayed some exercises, while the older girls danced. What I really liked was the dance – *The Insulted Bride*. But what left the greatest impression on me was the dance routine *Yellow Star*, created and organized by the ballet master Nina Gerstein. I cannot forget it, it is always in front of my eyes.

A little girl runs onto the stage. She dances joyously, carefree, just like a pretty butterfly. Suddenly it gets dark. From above an immense six-pointed yellow star slides down. The music is awe-inspiring, gloomy. The girl is frightened. In the background is a black curtain and so the star definitely seems so terrifying, just like a large hiding spider. The girl wants to run, to escape. She is rushing all over, begging, scared, but it is all in vain, she just falls down as if mown over. It would have been more accurate if they would have shown a swastika in the form of a spider, but everyone understood the meaning anyway. It was particularly the swastika that is compelling us to wear this yellow star.

In the surrounding regions – Asmena,[78] Mikhalishki[79] and others – *aktions* occurred. About 3,000 persons were shot.

Another 3,000. So far tens of thousands, hundreds of thousands were killed!

The ghettos were completely liquidated in these places. The German officers feel that at the present there are swarms of partisans in the surrounding forests, and that the Jews living not far from these forests, in small localities, will unconditionally join the partisans. For this reason the Jews are relocated to the Vilnius and Kaunas ghettos.

It looks like on this occasion they were definitely being relocated. The ghetto police were sent there and they are supposed to implement a registration.

---

[78] Also known as Ashmyany; a city in present-day Grodnenski Province, Belarus Republic, about 30 miles from Vilnius.
[79] A city in present-day Grodnenski Province, Belarus Republic, not far from Asmena.

Yesterday they sent several regiments of ghetto police there to bring them here.

Today the first migrants arrived, they were brought in wagons. Every second wagon was accompanied by an armed German soldier.

They are counted as they enter the ghetto. In addition to this, they are not arbitrarily released, but in groups. So far they are not far from the ghetto, on Arklu St.

They were deceived.

Of all those driven to Kaunas only a few men survived. They were clandestinely smuggled into the ghetto and then explained the unbelievable truth. Initially all went normal. They were taken by train. The cars rushed along like a long screened snake. They drove by fields, forests, stations and substations.

All were calm. They guessed along the way, "How will life be in Kaunas?" If the future is unknown it seems to be similar to the past. And this past recollected in our memories

Suddenly the train started to reduce its speed. The forest! Pits! And German soldiers.

They rushed to break the security bars on the windows. Others cried like captives, beating against the walls of the cars with their fists. Out of those cars where guards sat at the doors the men pushed them aside and jumped out. The ran wherever they could, in every direction, some directly into the forests, others along some trail, a third group through the fields. The guards started to shoot. The executioners who were waiting at the pits ran here. Nevertheless people jumped from the cars and ran. Young people, old people, women, children, no one stayed in the cars. The wounded fell, the healthy attacked the soldiers, grabbing their machine guns from them, suffocated them, but they were shot anyway, mown down by bullets. The wounded writhed in pain, calling for help. Others, insane from the terror and pain, begged to be relieved of their misery. The soldiers cursed at them, they wrapped each other's bitten hands, chased the unfortunates along the roads, fields and ditches. They stumbled over the wounded and dead, piercing their bayonets into the groaning. But they could not stop the situation: all were still running from the cars. One soldier rushed to the conductor and ordered him to move. But nothing could stop the people from escaping. One jumped from the moving train and fell under the wheels, another fell and broke his legs, while others just kept jumping.

Finishing up with all the escapees, the soldiers drug handfuls of old men and helpless women out of the cars who were packed into the corners. They herded them to the pits. In the forest again shots echoed.

All the trails had corpses scattered. The ditches were filled with them. Even in the meadow, and as far as the eye could see, corpses were decaying. It was not long ago that these were men full of life and joy, beautiful women, and children. Executioners walked among the bodies. Kicking them with their boots, hitting them with their rifle butts, turning them over. Suspecting that one was still alive, he would shove his bayonet into his stomach. They dug into their pockets, into dropped packages. Finding something of value they would shove it inside their undershirt.

Then they drove away. Only a few guards remained. They will guard the corpses.[80]

Night. The ground has a hard time breathing. The corpses of innocent people press on it.

At early morning the German officials ordered Gens to sent 25 ghetto policemen, to have them gather the corpses and discard them into the pits. Those that died on the rails had to be moved off, and which caused the train to be an hour late, but they still needed to be gathered and taken to the pit.

---

[80] April 4-5, 1943, some 5,000 were shot.

The task of the ghetto police was openly announced to the public. This was so we would know: it is foolish to try to resist or flee.

The ghetto police driven there are also under strict guard. They are depressed and bewildered. It is not only unpleasant to have to haul corpses, but also terrifying. The fascists do not like to leave witnesses to their crimes.

Just before evening several wagons full of the clothes from the executed entered the ghetto.

We all know that they are executed naked. But it was news to us that their clothing was taken someplace from Ponary. But they never brought it into our ghetto, we never saw any of it. But if our eyes do not see it directly, it is not so depressing.

The wagon maneuvers along the narrow pavement. The clothing flutters as though alive. Sleeves hang over the side. Yesterday morning a person got dressed, shoved his hands through the sleeves. But now this hand is long cold. A child's jacket. How old was this child, the one who wore it? A hat. Maybe it covered a severed head before it was taken. The hat slides off. Under it a boot is sticking out.

I want to cry, howl, bite, sob. Just yesterday, yes, it was just yesterday that a heart was beating under these clothes, a warm body was breathing! Just yesterday these were genuine persons! But now they are not! They killed them! Do you hear – killed them!

The ghetto police returned late. Their appearance was dreadful. One returned unconscious. He recognized his mother as a mutilated corpse with its head crushed.

They are almost saying nothing about it. They only informed us that there were many corpses and they did not have enough time to gather them all, and so tomorrow they need to return and continue.

Different ghetto police were sent to gather the remaining corpses.

The ghetto is immersed into mourning.

Murer is being transferred. Everyone is wishing that he be hung by the neck somewhere along the road to his new position. No one yet knows whom they will assign to his post.[81]

Kittel[82] was assigned in Murer's place. He is already credited for his cruelty, having annihilated several ghettos and work camps. They say he was a decorator at a movie theater. He exchanged his profession for the vocation of an executioner.

What has evolved from this is that the *aktions* and cruelty of Murer were meager in comparison to what is now awaiting us.

The ghetto is troubled. Some are gathering to somehow migrate to the partisans; others are searching for their friends in the city, perhaps to hide there; a third group prepares to shelter themselves within the ghetto.

Murer is no longer here. Prior to his departure he was in the ghetto. We feared that he might impose a bloody *aktion* as part of his farewell gesture, but fortunately he was subdued. No one knows why he even came here.

The mood is dreadful. Kittel is getting ready to begin his reign with a castration of the men.

The optimists are attempting to inspire hope, that he, after reviewing the matter, will not accept the position and will request Berlin if he can change his mind and hope they will grant this.

No one believes the comforters and everyone wanders around depressed.

I have written nothing for a long while. If it is not the heat to blame then it is my mood. True, there is no special news to report. But now I am writing at dawn of a very restless and

---

[81] June 29, 1943
[82] Bruno Kittel, 1922- ?. He is credited as being the liquidator of the ghettos of Riga, Vilnius and Kaunas.

sleepless night. What awaits us today is unknown. Maybe this comment will be the last. Kittel is threatened to liquidate the ghetto. But I will describe it all in order.

The night began very restless. We knew nothing that was definite, but one fact is that all the night excursions were cancelled and no one, with the exception of the ghetto police, has the right to appear on the street. This is all a premonition of nothing good to happen.

A neighbor dared to go outside, he should have known better.

Leaning against the windows we also attempted to see, hear, understand, something. But we only heard distant and nearby police blowing their whistles, the sound of their boots against the pavement, profanity. Some gunshots were noticed. Someone cried. Ran. The footsteps faded.

Finally the neighbor returned. He brought very sad news. An underground group of communist party members was discovered in the city. Their tracks led to the ghetto. The Gestapo ordered Gens to arrest I. Wittenberg,[83] a member of the communist party in the city. (He appears to be the leader of the FPO.)

Gens summoned Wittenberg to his office, and he, not knowing why he was being summoned, went. Gens arrested him and handed him over to the waiting city police. But when Wittenberg was being led through the ghetto, partisan associates attacked the police with their weapons, freed their commander and hid. Among those who freed him was this tree-cutter whom I knew face to face. So he was a member of the FPO! (This was S. Kaplinski, recently the commander of the partisan regiment *For Victory*.)

Such a failure caused Gens to go insane. Together with his policemen he is running, searching. The reason is that the Gestapo served him an ultimatum, that if they do not deliver Wittenberg, they will liquidate the ghetto. And this will also be

---

[83] Isack Vittenberg, 1907-1943.

the end for Gens and all of his police. This is why they are
frantically crawling out of their skin to find him.

Soon it will be morning. I am finishing writing. Will they
release me for work or not?

I have just returned from work. The news is bad.
Wittenberg is at the Gestapo office.

Now I learned the events of the night and day in detail.

Once finding out about Wittenberg's arrest the ghetto
partisans started to relay through their communication chain
their password *Lisa calls*, which means a prompt mobilization
and readiness of all the members of the FPO for fighting.

(One girl whose name was Lisa, a member of the FPO –
although I never learned her surname – was arrested upon her
attempt to smuggle weapons into the ghetto. She was shot. The
name *Lisa* became a symbol of the struggle.)

Gens' attempts to again find Wittenberg were futile. The
armed ghetto partisans resisted the several attempts of the
ghetto police to get near the building where they were
barricaded.

Gens decided to change his tactics. He ordered them to
relate the Gestapo's ultimatum to Wittenberg: either
Wittenberg or the entire ghetto.

Quickly Gens' intermediary returned with an answer: The
partisan organization does not feel that Wittenberg's delivery
can save the ghetto. If Kittel has already issued the order to
liquidate, this means, he will liquidate it. And the partisans
will resist, they will fight against the fascists. And Wittenberg,
their commander, will lead the defense.

In short, the Gestapo will not get Wittenberg.

And time ruthlessly proceeded forward. Gens again sent an
intermediary.

And suddenly Wittenberg announced that he will turn
himself in. He does not want to be the cause of the death of
20,000 persons. He bid farewell to his comrades, requested

them to continue the struggle, and voluntarily went to Gens' office, where the Gestapo officers were supposed to soon arrive.

At the outside of the ghetto, at the entrance to the house where Gens lived, a covered automobile belonging to the Gestapo stopped. When Gens led Wittenberg out, armed guards immediately grabbed him and shoved him into the car. They punched it.

They will surely torture Wittenberg and then kill him.

I do not know how long I will myself live, but I need to be grateful to Wittenberg for what he did. Today he saved me. Not only me, but mama, Miriam, the children and thousands of mothers and children.

It appears that Wittenberg had poison on his person, and he poisoned himself at Gestapo offices.[84]

The neighbor supposes that they were not able to track down the entire underground [communist] group in the city. Apparently Wittenberg was not the only one to join the gorkom[85] from among those in the ghetto. Since others were not demanded, this means they did not know about any others. But of course they will continue to search for partisans.

A large regiment of the members of the ghetto FPO departed into the forest to become partisans. It was essentially those who were seen with weapons in their hands during the search for Wittenberg. To remain in the ghetto now would have been twice as dangerous.

Another day, more news. In connection with the issue of people leaving to join the partisans Gens ordered all the brigadiers to present to the guard at the gates a list of all the members of his brigade, and every day, morning and evening, to inform him of how many persons were leaving the ghetto for work and how many were returning.

---

[84] August 16, 1943
[85] Communist city committee

Recently in the city they caught one member of the FPO, Svirski, they found a weapon on him and hauled him to Lukiskes prison. They also brought his two daughters there from the ghetto also. When the soldiers came to the cell to get the father, the younger one threw herself at him, embraced his neck with both her arms and would not let him go. The soldier fired and the girl fell down dead on the floor of the cell. They took Svirski and the elder daughter to Ponary.

This morning one ghetto policeman who was assigned to guard the gates detained a young man who was attempting to bring a weapon into the ghetto. The young man asked him to release him, explaining that this weapon is for the struggle against German soldiers. He was convinced that this struggle should be of interest to all of them. He knew that in the end the German soldiers and ghetto police would not spare the residents. The policeman did not want to hear his excuses. He started to shout at him that because of his hot temper the entire ghetto will suffer. But if he will live calmly, work and not resist, the Germans will not do anything bad to him. "There is no way that you can defeat automatic weapons and tanks with just your revolver. Because of this revolver they can destroy the entire ghetto."

Having lost hope to discuss the issue in a nice way with the obstinate policeman the young man shot him and, taking advantage of the commotion, disappeared.

The wounded policeman was taken to the hospital. The ghetto authorities hurried there. They ordered the doctor to take all measures to save his life. But nothing could be done as the wound was fatal and the policeman had to say farewell to his life.

The previous night they softly knocked on our apartment. They were two ghetto policemen. Excusing themselves for the inconvenience they ordered our neighbor Kaufmann and his family to go with them to Gens' office. So Kaufmann and his wife go, they leave the baby with the grandmother. But quickly the policemen return and relayed a request from the parents to bring the baby. The aged woman warmly wrapped him and took him.

We started to worry. Once they come at night for the baby means that some danger is hanging over the ghetto, but Gens wants to save his own people. Kaufmann was friends with Gens, he was a brigadier of a group of workers at the *Heresbaushtel*, and a member of the "council of brigadiers" that Gens created.

The grandmother returned, but she could not tell us anything. She gave the baby to the mother. They were sitting in the building that housed the police department, and there were several other brigadiers with their families there. Why they were summoned, no one knew.

Morning finally came. The streets were totally calm, people were readying for work, while the brigades were to proceed without their brigadiers who were summoned to Gens' office. Someone will replace them for the one day.

In the evening, after returning from work, I found out.

What occurred is that a solid group of brigadiers with their families were gathered that night at the police department, and they got tired of waiting. And it was the commander of the workers' police, Tovbin, who gathered them all on behalf of Gens.

Just before morning Tovbin relayed Gens' request to move them all into the ghetto prison. The people became upset. What does this mean? But noticing how quiet the ghetto was they calmed. In addition to this, the supervisor of the prison, Beigel, also assured them that nothing is threatening them. The brigadiers believed them and calmed.

But then they quickly heard from the city side of the ghetto, along Lidskaya St, an automobile driving up. On the staircase the footsteps of soldiers' boots could be heard and the voices of ghetto police. They were herding people out from the next cell.

They did not want to go and they explained why, but no one was listening to them. Then in the yard they heard Gens' voice. The brigadiers sat frightened, barely breathing.

(The prison had a secret passage directly into the city. The key to this metal grated gate was in the hands of the prison supervisor. Gens seldom utilized the gate, only in those circumstances when those sitting in jail had to be transferred to the occupiers secretly and away from the view of the ghetto residents.)

When the automobile drove away a smiling Beigel entered the cell. He informed them that the danger had passed. Soon they will be able to return home.

So what is it that happened?

It appears that Kittel demanded that the brigadiers, and specifically those supervising brigades where even one person escaped to join the partisans, be shot.

But because all of these brigadiers were associates of Gens, he gave him other people instead. Now the brigadiers will soon return home.

Suddenly again the noise of an arriving automobile was heard. It stopped. Soldiers are banging on the grated gate!

The scared Beigal opens it. An outraged Kittel rushes past him. He ordered them to immediately summon Gens.

Kittel screams at him, cusses at him, threatens him, that he will not tolerate such a deception, and demands the actual brigadiers.

Every word can be heard in the jail cell. Gens orders the door to be opened.

Kaufmann's wife runs to the window on the second floor. A grating is over it. The grandmother had been standing outside since early morning. The mother carefully squeezes the baby through the bars and hollers, "At least let him live," and then drops him. Pressing her crying grandchild close to her heart the aged woman ends up seeing her son and daughter-in-law off to death.[86]

They are no longer. Kittel communicated this himself. Just before evening he came to the ghetto and ordered everybody to attend an assembly and announced that just a few hours earlier in Ponary 32 persons were shot: 11 brigadiers and their families. The sentence of death was imposed on them because they poorly supervised the members of their brigades. "Let everyone know that beginning today, for every person who escapes into the forest and joins the partisans his entire family will be executed, the brigadier and the others *Juden* of this brigade. The authorities easily determine who escapes to join the partisans, because all of them are eventually caught along the road. Let the execution of 32 persons be a lesson for all of you. Let not the *Juden* blame someone else. They could have worked, meaning they could have lived, but they brought death upon themselves by taking this route." He, that is, Kittel, also added that he will not tolerate deceptions similar to this one, where in place of the actual brigadiers they inserted some aged men.

Boys are walking about the ghetto with placards. On them is written an announcement that tomorrow, on Sunday, at the hall at the theater, all the brigadiers and workers are summoned. Gens has an important message to deliver.

Gens explained the situation with the brigadiers in his address, what they already heard. He ordered them to watch for each other. If one more of them decides to join the partisans, they will not just shoot the escapee's family and brigadier, but the entire brigade. In order to make it easier for them to track one another the brigades will now be divided into groups of 10 persons. Every group of 10 will have a senior supervisor who will answer for the entire group. The

---

[86] Apparently the grandmother returned to the prison after she came home after delivering the baby to the mother.

individuals members must also be vigilant. If they discover or even suspect someone intending to leave and join the partisans, they are obligated to immediately report it.

"By doing this," said Gens, "they will save not just themselves, but the entire brigade."

We already have such groups in our brigade. Thank God that I am too young and nobody recommended me to become this senior. All rejected the offer, no one wants to take such a responsibility upon themselves.

August begins with good news: Orel and Belgorod are liberated! There was a parade in Moscow to celebrate.

How many cities are already liberated! But they are all distant from Vilnius. The adults say that the Red Army might reach here within 6 months, but no sooner. So another entire six months. And maybe even longer. No, no, not to think about it! Believe, just believe.

Kittel is not a human! A human cannot be so monstrously cruel!

He arrived at the Kenski peat camp[87] in a rather good mood, with an entire retinue and with gifts: cigarettes, tobacco and marmalade. He ordered the tobacco to be distributed to the best workers and the marmalade to go to their children. He inspected the camp and their work places. He asked if there was a barber in the camp and requested a shave.

The supervisor of the camp and the workers also could not at all understand what all of this meant. One person attempted to make a joke of it, that the German officials must be in bad straits if they need to visit the Jews as guests and even then with gifts. But the majority well remembered that they distributed ration cards for the best products just before an *aktion* at the ghetto. They viewed the situation distrustfully. Maybe the marmalade was poisoned?

---

[87] Peat was manufactured from plant and wood byproducts and used as fuel in homes. This labor camp was located near Vilnius.

But Kittel on this occasion involved himself in light conversation and expressed his positive hopes in regard to questions about another camp.

Finishing his tour and shave he ordered all the workers to be assembled in a warehouse where he was to deliver a speech.

In his address he ordered everyone to work hard and especially to not become involved with the partisans. The German authority is not making any plans at all to annihilate the Jews. They need their working strength. If they work they will live! But the German authority from their side will strive to better their working conditions and nourishment.

Although these statements seemed unbelievable they created a better mood for the gullible.

Finishing his address Kittel left for the door. He whistled and soldiers as though grew right out of the ground. After accompanying him out they closed the doors. The people started to worry, started to shout, bang on the walls and door. But no one would respond. Panic arose.

Each person rushed to the door hoping that they might be able to do something. All are crying, pushing each other. Some attempt to calm down, begging not to raise a panic and not display their fear. Maybe this isolation is just temporary, maybe they are planning for a search to verify that they have no weapons. Others are afraid that Kittel for sure wants to take the families and leave only the workers behind at the camp. Again a large clamor, cries, groans, threats and pleas start. People are attempting to push over the immense doors of the warehouse, to knock over the walls. But all is futile. The walls are solid and deaf to their pleas. The Germans outside are laughing and also deaf to their predicament.

Suddenly smoke is entering through slots. A fire!!! The pleas turn into wild cries. They are knocking with their fists with greater frenzy. People are climbing up to reach a balcony, they look for an exit through the roof.

The smoke is thickening. One young man removes his revolver and decides to use it, he shoots into the air. Once, again, a few more times. No response of any kind. But he has shot all his rounds, not even one remains to use on himself.

A flame can be seen. It is expanding, getting closer. They are struggling with the suffocating smoke. People are crying, calling for help. Maybe some women remaining in the barracks will hear them and run to save them.

The flame is not relenting, it is coming closer to them. Those along the edge of our crowd are trying to hide from the flames as they force their way toward the center of the building. But it is so tight, all are so densely packed one to another there is no where to move. The clothing and hair of some are already on fire. Insane from the pain they rush to the center where the fire has not yet reached. They cause others to burn. They also want to run away, escape. But where? In vain do they push against each other. In vain do they attempt to beat the flames off each other, they cry from the pain. Several persons have collapsed unconscious. Others are falling on them. The flames are raging worse, it is hurrying to envelop all of them, engulf them, cover them with its red fury.

Suddenly from the area of the barracks wild cries of women can be heard, cries for help. They are also on fire! And children, small children!!! The terror is more piercing due to the living losing consciousness.

The roof collapses, the walls fall. It is a massive bonfire of persons and timber.

While Kittel and his associates are standing not to far away on a small hill and enjoying the spectacle.

When he could watch no more he sat in his car and rushed away. He ordered the soldiers to watch that the flames do not migrate to nearby trees and not to leave the area until the bonfire burns itself out. Then they must mix the ashes up well. After the fire is finally finished they can then return to Vilnius.

The bonfire burned long. It took the soldiers a long while to mix the ashes with the pieces of burnt bones.

After the soldiers packed and left, the wind remained to finish the event. It played with the ashes, raising it and driving it away.

Only two persons survived. Noticing the preparations being made by the German soldiers they fled and hid in a canal, under a small bridge, until all the Germans left. Then they managed to return to the ghetto and told all about it.

Kittel also liquidated the Reshski peat camp.

This occurred because, they say, after an altercation with partisans in the forest the fascists found a hat and an identification card was located inside the lining and it had the name of a worker at the Reshski peat camp. It was easier for Kittel to liquidate this camp. He shot all the persons and buried them right there.

I heard they killed one member of the FPO – Tiktin. Of all of those located at Burbiskis,[88] he was alone able to pilfer some weapons from the German military outpost. Noticing that he was exposed he attempted to flee but an enemy bullet caught up to him.

What is now to happen? It is clear matters cannot continue this way much longer. The German officers can perfectly see that there are no longer obedient and scared people in the ghetto who can be deceived in every manner, and whom they can treat any way they want. Now all of them are resisting one way or another: the Wittenberg situation, the FPO, the massive exodus to the partisans, the Kaunas *aktion*, during which people with their bare hands defended themselves and attacked the guards.

No way will the fascists tolerate this. Someone is trying to assure us that they do not have the right to liquidate the large ghettos at their own discretion, without the consensus of the

---

[88] In north central Lithuania

higher authorities. But of course the higher authorities will unconditionally give them this permission. What is the Kenski camp, what is the Reshski, what is the Vilnius ghetto to them? They are all the same.

What will happen now?

Meanwhile they are all the more tightening our fetters. All those who employ *Juden* were sent instructions signed by the *Gebietskommissar*, as to how to deal with them. "It is absolutely necessary for them to make sure they do not walk without their stars or with a star poorly sewn to their clothing. No need to divide them into small group, but better for them to work alone. It is prohibited to release a *Juden* outside the limits of his work station, even if someone is to accompany him. It is absolutely necessary to isolate him from workers of other nationalities. If the minutest insubordination or dissatisfaction is noticed, you must immediately inform the German authorities. All privileges are prohibited. If there is a dining room at their place of work, the *Juden* is not just prohibited from eating there, but even from entering. For not observing these directives the supervisors of the companies will be liable and subject to the consequences."

Regardless the young people still leave to join the partisans.

Yesterday a man horribly scared and in dirty and torn clothes ran into the ghetto, he entered along with another group returning from work. He skipped into the yard of Building 7 on Rudninka Street. All who work at the airport live there.

He told them how suddenly that day they were surrounded by a large regiment of soldiers. They ordered them to stop work and get in formation. Fear overwhelmed them. However it was unthinkable to run, the guards surrounded them like a tight chain. Some German officer said that they are being taken to Estonia to work there.

No way did anyone believe any of it.[89]

Several other large brigades did not return from work either. The ghetto is like a cemetery.

The more time goes by the worse it is. Rumors spread that the Jews are being laid off from work everywhere. Some will remain only in a few places, but not many.

The incorrigible optimists nourish themselves with the assurance that this is impossible. As long as the ghetto exists, the occupiers will strive to utilize as much as possible the work strength available. They cannot arbitrarily liquidate the ghetto, they need approval. And the front is moving toward us at a fast pace that by the time they receive the approval the Red Army may already be so close that the Germans will not be thinking about the ghetto but about their own skin.

If it were only this way.

The *Arbeitsamt* has already received a list of companies where all the Jews are being laid off. Mama and I were also laid off from work.

Today is a very strange day. Due to habit all of us gathered in the street this morning, in our spots. We enviously stared at those few brigades who were nevertheless leaving for work.

More stayed than left. It is unusual to see at this time of day so many people standing here, especially men. There is nowhere to go, nothing to do. And there is nothing to eat.

It appears that hardship has no limits. It seems to us that it cannot get any worse. But maybe it can.

Tomorrow no one will leave for work, the last of us has been laid off. The ghetto will be closed, isolated from the rest of the world.

The night was calm.

---

[89] From August 6 to 24, 1943, about 7,000 were taken to Estonia.

This morning I heard that as if Gens assured us that all who were not working and still want to work will receive work, but not in the city but within the ghetto limits. The reason everyone was terminated from work was to make it impossible for any more to leave and join the partisans. The workshops will be expanded, especially the sewing and knitting. There will be three shifts. More military uniforms and linen is being received, and which needs to be washed and mended. The workshops are accepting new workers.

I work in the knitting section. It is quite large occupying the entire hall of the *Judenrat*. We sit 20 persons to the table. The supervisor brings a pile of torn gloves. We mend the fingers or palm and return them. We work in three shifts.

There is nothing to eat. They are more careful right now as to how many ration cards they are distributing, but so few! The further time progresses the harder it is to endure the hunger.

This is why it seems to me that the ghetto is now much like an old automobile where all the screws have been removed. As long as you don't touch it, it stays together, but should someone just lean their finger against it, it will crumble.

In the morning when we just started work (this week I work at the morning shift) a rumor circulated that the ghetto was surrounded. We wanted to stop work and run home, but the supervisor would not allow our shift to leave. He closed the door and ordered us to remain at our places. He will walk outside and ascertain the situation.

We wait. Of course, we are unable to further work. We are agitated, guessing, and all the while staring at the door.

Finally he returns. By the expression of his face we understood that the rumors were confirmed. We ran to our homes.

What are we to do? Where are we to go? If I hide in one place, they might quickly find me there, or if I hide somewhere else, I might survive.

Too late to do anything, the soldiers are already in the ghetto. We rush into the basement. It is damp here, smells like mold. In each wall there is a crawlspace, a tunnel into the next basement, another just like this one, and from there into a third. This basement apparently branches under all the buildings.

Others rushed here from different apartments. There are so many of us now. Cramped, dark, we move by touch. Children are crying. The more arriving are forcing us deeper into the basement, and only a few men remain on the stairs. They will overhear what is occurring upstairs.

In the darkness I lost mama and Ruvik. They are no doubt at the other end. I hold Rayechka tightly by the hand so at least not to lose her. Miriam remained at work at her workshop.

We are tired due to standing. We sit. It is cold, damp, at least our legs rest. I set Rayechka on my knees.

What is going on upstairs? Is the liquidation finishing, or just the next *aktion*?

Time drags on. It is quiet.

Some are talking, someone needs to climb out and go upstairs to find out what is going on.

It appears that a ghetto policeman is also in the basement with us. In the morning, scared by the general panic he also ran into the basement. It would be the least dangerous if he was to climb upstairs.

He cleaned his uniform best he could and after promising to quickly return he climbed out.

Much time has passed and he is not back. If the police are even being apprehended this means the liquidation is in process. The end...

Suddenly a knock is heard. No one answers. The knock repeats. The policeman is returning. The door opens for him. With an official and commanding tone of voice he orders everyone to climb out from the basement.

At the exit stand two ghetto policemen. They are letting the women and children through, but restraining the men. The [police] shout at them not to resist or else they will be shipped to Estonia to work.

But who believes them?

Terrifying cries and shouts start again. The men are running back into the basement, the police are chasing after them, catching them. They assemble them and bring them out.

I enter the street. Only a few soldiers are here, the ghetto police are wandering around. It appears that Gens was ordered to supply 3,000 men that are needed. The entire FPO is mobilized and located in several yards along Strashuno St ready for battle. The ghetto police know this and avoid these buildings, afraid of an altercation.

However for Gens to fulfill the order dictated by the occupiers is no so easy. The men have all hid. Gens himself is running yard to yard without a hat, without a jacket or insignia, so that people would voluntarily exit their shelters. He is not threatening them, but promising that they will be taken to Estonia to work. But if they do not exit, they will bring disaster on the entire ghetto.

No one is coming out; they have not believed him for a long while.

Soon it will be dark, and not even a thousand have been gathered. Gens is totally insane. He threatens the police: If they do not assemble the necessary quantity they will go themselves. Now they are furious.

They are running, chasing, shouting, beating. They run into the synagogue, which was a former apartment in the courthouse at the corner of Shyaulu and Mesino Streets, and drug out of there a dozen frightened aged men who were reciting prayers. They hauled them to the gates. There, it appears, was Kittel. Seeing the "products" they were handing him he reprimanded the police and ordered them to take the aged men back into the ghetto.

The police talk about this every step they take. You know, they say, a better reason to just put them to work.

At dusk they were only succeeded in getting 1,300 men, but they need 3,000.

A whistle blew. The *aktion* ended. The exhausted police were released to go home. But only until tomorrow. The ghetto remained surrounded.

Today was the same. The acquisition of men continued. Many were driven away, while several hundred were buried alive.

It is not known how the German soldiers found out that many men were hiding in the basement of Building 15 on Strashuno St. Entering the yard together with Gens the Germans using a loudspeaker announced that all those hiding in the basement of this building must immediately go into the yard. If they do not leave, there will be an explosion! Let the women save their husbands and brothers, let them convince them to come out. Gens repeated the same. All was futile. The minutes went by: one, two, five, but no one came out. The supervisor of the Germans ordered all the women to leave the building within five minutes. The soldiers started to prepare the explosive. They placed the explosives under the half of the building, where the basement was located.

A terrifying alarm arose among the women. Some hurried and ran out of the yard, others attempted to interfere with the soldiers planting the explosives, a third group ran like insane people to the basement and back, one shouting for the men to leave, one shouting for them to stay. Several who were more relaxed, stood at the entrance and chased away the alarmists: the basement was deep, made of concrete, and an explosion would not harm it.

Noticing that the soldiers are themselves running from the yard, the women likewise started to run.

A horrible explosion. I was standing at a distance and it almost blew me apart. The rock wall tilted, as though getting on its knees, and collapsed. A cloud of dust arose. When it somewhat settled the ruins could be seen. Half the building was as though it never was.

The women quickly rushed into the yard to dig into the basement. Each one drug what she could: bricks, boards, wire. New helpers hurried into the yard. I ran home to notify my mama where I was and then returned to help.

In one place we felt a body. We started to dig further. We unearthed a torso, an arm and a child's hand. I became nauseous and ran into the street. I returned only after the bodies of the mother and child, wrapped in a bed sheet, were taken to the morgue.

Suddenly behind our backs a German soldier surfaced. He prohibited us from digging. If people were not going to obey the orders of German officers they must die. He will shoot each of them personally, anyone who will dare get near or pick up even one brick.

But they still did not gather the required 3,000 by evening. Tomorrow the *aktion* will continue.

Today German officials exposed ghetto partisans, they were at the yard at Building 12 on Strashuno St. They threw some grenades into it. Then the fascists turned into raging animals and demolished the entire building, burying beneath its ruins not only the fighters, but the women and children residing there.

But the German soldiers ended up also paying for their lives. Gens did not know how to justify himself. He assured them that the ghetto had no partisans, but only obedient and hard workers. So he had to settle the matter with a few of these greenhorns.

With greater frenzy Gens started to arrest men. He gave the impression he did not notice that along with the men there were women dressed in men's clothing, their wives who did not want to separate from them. Not important, as long as the quantity was met!

Out of the strongest men and scoundrels he organized an assistant police force, which not only helped the police apprehend people, but most important, guarded the sports field, where the members of the FPO were in custody, and not to let any of them to escape. Gens ordered them not to allow them to communicate with the residents of the ghetto, so they could not get them agitated and so rise against the Germans. He was afraid of an uprising, a genuine armed altercation with killers.

Finally the four-day *aktion* ended. The ghetto was no longer surrounded.[90]

Today on the final day, Braudo, one of Gens' friends, was arrested. He was connected with both the ghetto and the city *Arbeitsamt*.

During these days he also ran, ordered, apprehended, retained. Today, noticing not far from him a group of Germans, wanted to play a game with them. He pulled a rope or lash out of the leg of his boot and threw it at something. But when he was pulling out the lash he dropped some papers on the ground. The German soldiers stopped him and ordered him to show them the papers. Braudo attempted to talk them out of it, diverting them from them, but the German soldiers did not want to hear him. He had to show them. These were documents in some other name and another nationality. The fascists beat him up and shoved him into a truck filled with other arrests. The intervention of Gens did not help him. On the contrary the German soldiers made a thorough investigation whether he may have escaped from somewhere.

The *aktion* ended. The guard was removed. Now what is next?

---

[90] September 1-4, 1943

It is now September. The beginning of the school year, and again without me. No doubt they have forgotten me at school, or count me as gone.

Gens assigned the strongest policemen and almost the entirety of the assistant police force to Rasa St, where as with the previous occasion they hold apprehended persons in custody until their transfer to Estonia. The police are needed to help load them into railroad cars.

But they soon returned; the cars will arrived tomorrow.

The news is that all the men are alive and waiting for trucks, the ghetto is just a little upset, but nonetheless it is in some kind of stupor due to despair.

The ghetto police are back at Rasa St. Having returned they told us that all were loaded into a convoy, which will leave tonight for Estonia.

The police also brought more but bad news. They heard that at the railway station a sign was hung, or will be hung soon, having the inscription: *Juden frei*. This means that there are no more Jews in the city.

Yesterday they shot Gens.[91] We heard about it only today, but yesterday about noon we felt some kind of restlessness in the area. Someone said that a messenger from Noigeboer confiscated Gens' and Desler's weapons – two revolvers and some grenades, which they received for use in their police service.

Gens was summoned to the Gestapo.

It became dark. He still did not return. In the morning we found out that they shot him.

Where and how he was shot, no one knows. But they say that it was not at Ponary. No one feels sorry for him, maybe only some policemen.

---

[91] September 14, 1943

Although he was privileged, although he served the occupation zealously, nonetheless he could not escape our common fate.

The one and the same repeats: the German officials never leave behind either their accomplices or the witnesses of their crimes.

That he was an accomplice is a fact, otherwise they would not have trusted him so much and he would not have utilized different privileges. He had the right to walk about the city without stars and on the sidewalk. He was able to not just visit but also spend the night at his old apartment in the city, and where his wife and daughter still live, although the daughter was supposed to live at the ghetto. His wife is a Lithuanian. Based on the German race theory, even the third generation of a mixed marriage with a Jew is consider part-Jew.

Anyway, somehow Gens did not satisfy the fascists.

Our neighbor in the first room assures us that if Gens did not deceive people by trying to convince them that only through obedience could they escape Ponary and await liberation, and nothing would be accomplished through resistance, then the residents of the ghetto would have more actively become involved in the struggle against the occupiers.

All the furniture and belongings were removed from Gens apartment. The ghetto is without a president. Desler will probably be designated. He is nevertheless the eldest capable.

Pathetically though we will inherit the most unwanted person as president – Kittel. He has ordered the office to be furnished and himself selected the furniture and ordered it to be remodeled.

The German troops are being fought back at the front. The Red Army is approaching Smolensk. So it will not be long until liberation!

Somehow Miriam succeeded in escaping from the ghetto. She hopes that good people will hide her or provide her false documents. Maybe she will succeed in getting us out of here.

Again...

Kittel has demanded 1,000 men for work in Estonia. All occurred all over again. The soldiers surrounded the ghetto, while the police seized people.

About noon we found out that Desler escaped with his wife, he emptied the ghetto bank as well. Levas, the commander of the guards at the gate, also disappeared.

This means matters are very bad.

Kittel with his retinue are strolling through the ghetto. The streets are empty. We sit behind locked doors and curtained windows. It is only through a crack do we decide to observe the Gestapo.

During the day Kittel ordered lunch to be served him. He drinks with his retinue, while the police seize men. But now it is more difficult as no one want to obey his orders.

Just before evening Kittel walked out of his office. Some of the participating commanders contritely requested him to continue the *aktion* one more day, because they had not succeeded in gathering the demanded quantity of men. But Kittel informed them that he decided to cancel the *aktion*. The men in custody were to be released to go home.

After giving orders to seal Deslar's apartment Kittel left. He also cancelled the guard surrounding the ghetto.

A difficult and restless night descended on us.

It is quiet. Not one German soldier is in the ghetto. Apparently because it is Sunday. The gates are solidly locked. No one enters, no one exits. If they wanted us to live this way then don't even give us any food! Somehow we would manage. Very soon the Red Army will arrive here.

Kittel is back in the ghetto. In place of Desler Oberhart was assigned as chief of police.

They brought ten truckloads of jackets and gloves. They say that there are seven railway cars full standing at the station. If they are preparing to liquidate the ghetto they would not be bringing us new work.

It is a late September evening. Fear as heavy as lead has again fettered us. Still nothing has occurred, there is not one German soldier in the ghetto, still the residents are agitated.

At night at the sewing workshop, where the night shift worked, Oberhart came and ordered us to sew a special patch for his uniform. He waited until it was ready and then left wearing it on his arm. He did not talk otherwise, but we felt he was not his regular self.

Dawn. An overcast day. The ghetto is in an upheaval. People with their children and bundles are crawling into shelters. This time the police issued a general alarm. But this only caused the panic and fear to get worse.

Kittel arrived with several Gestapo. Oberhart met them at the gates and accompanied them to the office of the *Judenrat*. Along the route he ordered the police, who were still at their posts, to summon all the residents of the ghetto for an important announcement.

I ran there also.

The German officials walked to the porch of Desler's apartment. They asked for a megaphone. One read a directive of the chief of the Gestapo that the Jews of Vilnius ghetto, who were located here two years ago, will be evacuated to the worker's camps: one is in Estonia, another is here in Lithuania, not far from Siauliai. The evacuation will occur over the course of one day. You can only take with you as many items as you can carry.

He then added on his own, that he advises us to take a bucket, pots and other kitchen utensils, because we will not be provided this at the new location. We need to be ready within four hours.

After explaining it once, he read the directive a second time. Then Oberhart twice repeated it in Hebrew.

Done. Now we need to go home and assemble on Rudninka Street at 11 o'clock.[92]

I bring mama the bad news. Rayechka looks at us with her scared face, "And maybe they are not telling us the truth and are hauling us to Ponary?" How should I answer her? That I also think the same?

Mama orders the children to empty their briefcases, she will put some linen for each of us in them.

"So we will not take our books?" Ruvik asks frighteningly. "They will not allow us to read there?"

"If you have spare time, child, you will read," mama comforts him. But her voice is shaking so hard that Ruvik very distrustfully stares at her.

Mama assembles the things. The children sit on the bunk shivering and timidly watch her. Seeing that she is crying they also blink with their large eyes.

Attempting to convince them that there is no need to weep, that maybe they will be taking us to this camp. Even if it will be worse there, somehow we will endure. There is not long to wait until the liberation. But I do not believe myself that this camp exists and my words do not provide any comfort.

I stand at the widow. It is dirty outside. This spring it will be dry. But not only here, everywhere. The apple blossoms will soon turn the area white. The wind will blow the petals away as though they are alive and give its fragrance. And the sky will be blue as blue can be. And infinity is so big. How nice it would be to stare at it! Or to attach myself to the filaments on the flowers. I would have so much reason to be happy if I was to remain alive.

Mama says it is time to leave.

[92] September 23-24, 1943

The streets are packed with people. Silent, gloomy, migrating in the same direction toward Rudninka St. Some are dragging large bundles, others walk with next to nothing. Maybe this is the intelligent thing to do: Why burden yourself at your final hours?

I carry a suitcase, a bundle, and over my shoulder is papa's autumn coat that the teacher Jonaitis brought a while back to the ghetto gates. Mama still did not decide to sell it, she was saving it "for the bleakest day."

There is chaos on Rudninka St. Apparently all are on their way. If this is the liquidation there is no reason to remain in some shelter. The Germans will no doubt resort to those same measures they used after the liquidation of the second ghetto. Water was cut off in that area, guards were placed everywhere. Tormented by thirst they left the shelters and were seized. The remaining died due to lack of water.

We are approaching the gates. How many times did I pass through here over the past two years. Will I ever return here? Will I ever see these buildings, windows, the church steeples towering on the other side of the gates?

Noigeboer, Kittel, Vais and some other Gestapo personnel stand at the exit. They are counting those exiting. So far a thousand, they add four more to the amount and we exit.

On both sides of the street, along the sidewalks, stand soldiers with dogs. You will not be able to slither through.

We wind our way along Etmanskaya St, cross Bolshaya, and turn on Subachayus. Here is the Philharmonic. Here is where our school choir would perform in contests.

We walk along Subachayus St. I have no strength remaining to drag my things. Papa's coat keeps sliding off my shoulder. Obviously it is not only difficult for me, discarded bundles wallow in the mud. It is harder to walk because of them, I need to jump over or walk around them. But I have no more strength. Mama orders me to discard the coat, but I cannot. I feel I would discard what is left of my father.

The coat slides off anyway. I want to pick it up, but someone steps on the sleeve. I attempt to stretch to get it, but now people are shouting at me, that there is no reason to get upset over a rag. Mama tells me not to get behind, otherwise I will get lost.

The coat is left behind. They mercilessly trample on it.

We stop not far from Rasa St. A jam. Those ahead are almost not moving, while those behind are walking on us.

What has happened? They could not be shooting people right here in the city. Maybe they are loading us into trucks.

It appears they are herding us though some gates, they go behind a Catholic Church. The men are remaining here, in the street, they are leading only a few forward into the yard, the women and children.

The wives, bidding farewell, weep, they wish their husbands a long life (no doubt they will take them to work somewhere). A couple walking next to us say good-bye in an unusually calm manner – they clasp each others hand and separate as if they will see each other soon. A young woman attempts to go backward. She is holding men's clothing in her hands. Looks like she wants to change clothes here in the crowd and go with her husband.

The yard is large. It is filled with soldiers. They are placing the sick brought from the hospital on the grass. Some lie right on the ground, others remain on their gurneys. Of course, after an operation or if they are paralyzed they cannot walk on their own. Among them circulate, and not knowing where to go, orphans from the orphanage, blue from the cold. The poor souls with their shaved heads shivering in their pitiful pajamas.

The herd us further, toward a ravine. And soldiers also surround it. And then even further, where on the other the other side of the ravine there is a narrow road. Soldiers stand near each house and on the roofs with machine guns.

This means it will be here, in this very village.

Our feet stick to the mud and we can barely get them out. Trudging along we approach the soldiers. One raises his automatic rifle. No, he is just indicating that we need to walk further. I guess they will shoot us in the back. To look back is scary. If it should only go straight into my heart!

Nevertheless I look back. The soldiers still stand where they were. Indifferently evil.

More people are being herded into the ravine. We are tired of standing. I release my suitcase into the mud. Mama says nothing. Her and I sit on our suitcases. We set the children on our laps.

An unending stream stretches from the ghetto. The intolerable rain does not stop not for a minute. We are thoroughly drenched. It flows off our hair, from our nose, from our sleeves. Mama orders the children to lift their feet higher so they do not get soaked. Next to us another mother is building a tent for her children: she stuck some sticks into the ground and covered it with a coat. How strange at such a time to be scared of catching a cold.

Mama sobs. I beg her, for the sake of the children, to be calm. But she cannot. She just looks at us and sobs even worse.

And people are still coming and coming. We thought there were less than this many in the ghetto. It will soon be dark. It is already crowded in the ravine. Some sit right where they are, others walk for some reason, wander, stepping over people and bundles. It is apparent they lost their own.

It is getting dark. But still somewhat visible, I will look at the trees, the birds' nests, branches, at the distant houses, at each of their windows. I guess I will no more see any of this. All is alive: every leaf, drop of rain, even the tiniest gnat. It will be living tomorrow, while we will be no more. No! I will not go to Ponary! I will remain here! I will bury myself in the ground, but I will not go anywhere! I do not want to die!

But I guess that those who were earlier shot also did not want to...

It is dark. The rain continues. Time to time the guards will illuminate us with flares. They guard us so we do not escape. But how can someone escape with so many of them?

Ruvik is shaking, maybe a nightmare. He fell asleep tucked into my shoulder. His warm breath tickles my neck. It is his last sleep. And there is nothing I can do for this warm breathing little body of his to not lie in a cramped pit that is slippery due to blood. Others will be piled over him. Maybe it will even be me.

Again they shoot a flare. It awakens Ruvik. He opens his eyes wide, he looks around frightened. He deeply, and not at all like a child, sighs.

Rayechka is not sleeping. She has totally exhausted mama with her questions, "Will they herd us to Ponary? Will we walk or will they take us on trucks? Maybe they just might take us to some camp? And when they shoot us, will it hurt?" Mama answers something through her tears. Rayechka caresses her, calms and, after thinking a bit more, again asks about something.

One more flare illuminated the ravine, the adjoining streets, the cold soldiers.

There is no way for me to escape, or mama or the children. None at all. If I walk away they will shoot me. So why do I waste my time thinking about this? Why am I torturing myself? I will get over the horror. Only initially when they herd us and then we will stand on the edge of the pit. After that I will not feel anything. It is horrifying for a living person to look at corpses, but they feel nothing.

Mama is still sobbing. "Children like these need to be given away, children like these." The night stretches so slowly...

Finally the darkness starts to noticeable melt. No doubt they will soon lead us further."

It is already almost light. Someone dared asked a guard, why we are being held here. He did not answer the question but said that they did not have enough time to clean out the ghetto, and so there are more to be brought today.

A sparrow sat on a branch very close to us. It turned its head, looked around and flew away. It flew in the direction of the direction of the guards. The sparrow can do that.

They brought new persons from the ghetto. Among them were seven policemen. They even retained the policemen at the gates just as the other men. Nonetheless they did not escape our common fate.

One of those who just arrived sat next to us. She saw above us, in this yard, two men and one girl who were hanged, ghetto partisans. They were isolated in the city, not wanting to give themselves up, so they shot back. They killed one German soldier and wounded a few. But there were more fascists. They surrounded the partisans and wrestled the weapons out of their hands, and brought them here shackled for execution. They said that the killed German soldier, whose name was Gross, was researching the activities of the partisans.

All three partisans encountered death heroically, raising their heads high, smiling. Even the girl, and still so young, she looked right in the eyes of her executioner with contempt and spat in his face. She turned to the ravine, let them all see that she was smiling!

Those sitting closer were able to recognize them: These were: Asya Big, I. Kaplan, and A. Khoinik.

The guards order us to stand and climb higher, into this yard. Our things are sopping wet, dirt sticking all over them. But we don't need them. Nevertheless I took my suitcase, but I left the bundle buried in the mud.

The yard is a packed crowd. Barely can we move to the doors on the other side. The closer we get the greater the pressure. Maybe they are not letting us out? More and even more ascend from the ravine. Will this yard hold so many? They have totally crushed us.

What is going on at the doors? Are they killing? Shackling? Or just slowly getting people into trucks?

It appears the doors are closed. They are letting people out only through a small grated gate. We approach, they are letting people through one by one. Mama is upset, she does not want to lose us and orders me to go first. Ruvik will follow behind me and Rayechka behind him, and mama will be last. This way she can see all of us.

I walk out. A soldier grabs me and pushes me to the side. I do not see any vehicles there. I turn to tell mama about this but she is not there. Across the street is a line of soldiers. Behind them is another, and further is a large crowd. I see mama there. I run to a soldier and ask him to let me go there. I explain that there is a misunderstanding, I was separated from my mother. She is standing over there. My mother is over there, I want to be with her.

I talk, I beg, but the soldier does not even hear me. I look at those women entering through the grated gate and now and then they will push one, then another, to my side. The remaining are herded there, toward the crowd.

Suddenly I hear mama's voice. She is shouting at me, not to go to her. And she is telling the soldier not to release me, because I am still young and have the ability to work well...

Still afraid to accept the truth of what is happening. I scream with all my strength, "Then you come to me! Come here, mama!" But she is shaking her head and with a distant and hoarse voice she cries, "Live, my child! At least you will be the one to survive! Be revengeful for the sake of the children!" She bends down to them, says something and picks them up, as heavy as they are, one by one, for me to see them. Ruvik stares with this blank expression, he is waving his hand...

They push them along. I see them no more.

I climb on a rock near the wall and gaze around, but mama is nowhere, not anywhere.

Where is mama? My eyes are in circles. Apparently from the pressure. I hear ringing in my ears, a howl. Why is this stream in the street? This is not a stream, it is blood.[93] There is a lot of it. It is foaming. But Ruvik is waving his hand motioning good-bye to me. But there is no way I can stretch my hand to him. Why am I rocking? I guess the rock I am standing on is sinking... I am sinking.

Why am I lying here? Where did the river disappear? There is no stream. I lie on the sidewalk. Several women lean over me. One is holding my head, another is checking my pulse.

Where is mama? I must see mama! But the women are not allowing me to stand. I fainted. This never happened to me before.

Kittel with Vais and some various Gestapo officers arrive. The women quickly get me on my feet. The German officers survey us and order us to stand in rows of ten.

They count us. Several times. Apparently they are making errors. Kittel shouts at the soldiers standing at the gate for them to add another seven to us, and that will be enough. All the remaining will be routed to the left.

There are 1,700 of us. We move. I turn my head in the direction of where mama and the children last stood. More are entering through the grated gate.

They lead us along Rasa St. We are brought into a large yard, obviously not far from the railroad station, as here are rails and box cars.

They count us in groups of 80 and put us in front of the boxcars. You must not move from your spot, they will shoot you.

Railway workers are busy near the boxcars. Some are inspecting, checking the wheels, other just plainly stare at us.

---

[93] She is hallucinating.

Some of the more daring girls quietly ask them if they know where we will be taken. They shrug their shoulders, others scared turn away hoping a guard did not notice him talking to us, a third group tries to calm us. Then this one young man laughs at us, saying that we will be taken to Ponary. He acts like he will be the one to drive us there.

Finally they open the boxcar doors and order us to get in. The cars are very high above the ground, and it is difficult for us to climb in, we drag each other by the hand. But the soldiers are in a hurry, they are beating us, ordering us to speed up. The boxcar is packed full, but they are shoving more in. The soldiers take their own measures to bring order: they beat us on the head with their rifle butts, they kick our feet to pack us in more.

One German soldier walks over, moves the door and closes it with a locking bar

It is dark. Just below the ceiling there are a few windows and with bars over them. One woman in the corner is asphyxiated, "Even horses are not packed so tightly in such cars when they are transferred." And again quiet. German soldiers walk parallel to the convoy, they shout something, order someone. The rain beats annoyingly.

Where is mama right now? What will they do with all of them? Maybe they will divide them once more. I doubt it. Didn't this railway worker say they are taking us to Ponary? So why did they have this selection? No doubt because there were not enough cars to take everybody at the same time, and so decided to play this joke on us. And tomorrow, recovering from their hangover, they will brag to each other how cleverly they fooled us. They selected the most healthy, young, but we the stupid ones believed that they are taking us to work. I weep. What have I done? What did mama do? Other people? Can they really kill us just because of nationality? Where did they acquire this barbaric hate toward us? Why?

The car jerked forward. We are traveling. And mama? Where is she? Why did they separate us? Death would not be so terrible if I was next to her.

We are getting further from Vilnius.

The women start to talk that the train is slowing. Ponary!

Women sitting closest to a window lifted one girl. She confirmed that we were at a forest. The convoy guards release flares from the train station and illuminate the forest. The wires fences are visible. In the distance between the trees something has a yellow tint. Maybe the sand in the pit? The train inches forward. Right now it will stop. This is the day of my death: September 24, 1943. No! I will not go! Let them shoot me right here, but I will not go there!

It jerked. Did it stop? No! It is still traveling. It is gaining speed. Away from Ponary?

We are again traveling. The wheels knock, they are taking us further from Vilnius, from mama. Where is she now?

Night. Another long dark night. If I could only for at least a minute stretch my swollen feet.

Light is penetrating the windows. It is dawn. The train is stopping. It is possible to ask for some water? I need to drink.

Again we are traveling. I am asphyxiated, hot and my health is now so poor. If the wheels did not knock so loud maybe we could summon the convoy guard and ask for some water. Maybe for just a minute he would open the door and allow just a drop of fresh air to enter. We are suffocating.

The train is again stopping. It is obvious this is a large city. A large crowd can be heard at the train station.

People are walking by the convoy. We knock on the walls with our fists, for them to open the door. No response. The girls lifted to the windows beg each railway worker walking by for even a drop of water. But they just shrug their shoulders and motion that the convoy guards do not allow it.

Unexpectedly someone walks to the doors and moves them open. Air!

It is a convoy guard. He bellows at us, for us not to holler. If he should hear even one more sound he will shoot us all!

It is no doubt long past noon, and the train is still standing. One thing we do know is that we are in Siauliai. Maybe there really is a camp here.

One woman proposed that we throw a note outside through the window. She passed out a stack of paper, with a pencil I write in four languages who we are, where we are from, and when we left. Maybe someone will find them and search for us.

It is getting dark and we are still here. My feet are in terrible pain. I feel like they will break at the knees.

Just before morning the train starts to move. Again we are traveling. But where?

Soon again we stop. But we did not attempt to figure where we were. In general some strange silence hovered. It was as if no one had any strength remaining to either cry or talk. Not even to think.

So the entire long day the train sat more than it traveled.

At night it stopped at some forest, but immediately again left. That night it rushed at an insane speed.

Again it stopped. Initially we did not pay attention. Then we suddenly shuddered; they are speaking in German? And dogs are barking!

Someone moved the door open and blinded us with flashlights. He circled the walls and corners and then shouted, "*Heraus*," meaning, "Get out!" The first were not even fast enough to jump out by the time soldiers were able to climb in and start to hit, shove and force us out. My feet were swollen to double their size and heavy as lead after sitting in such conditions for so long.

They pushed me also. Fortunately I fell on my hands. One soldier threw my suitcase at me, painfully striking my back. I barely stood up.

It was this same scene in each boxcar.

They arranged us. Here in the forest. The steam locomotive whistled, jerked its cars and pulled them after it. It sped away. No doubt back to Vilnius. It left us here in a foreign forest.

They herded us along a trampled trail. It was illuminated. The lights were not masked. In the distance more lights were seen, also unmasked. They illuminated a barbed wire fence. A sentry opens the gates.

The camp! Barracks. They are long, wooden, single-story. The windows penetrated a weak light. People were wandering about. All of them for some reason were wearing striped pajamas. Something strange was occurring at one barrack: these striped people were jumping out of the windows. They jump out and run back in and again appear at the windows and again jump. Meanwhile the German soldiers are beating them, hurrying them. The people fall, get hit, get up, again jump out. What is this? Are the fascists vilely mocking the insane?

We are ordered to place all our belongings in one pile on a square in front of a barrack. They will not allow us to take our things into the barrack.

Two soldiers guard the square. Here several men dressed in men's striped clothes aimlessly wander. The quiet ask where we came from. We also want to know where we ended. It appears we are not far from Riga, at the Kaiserwald concentration camp.[94] If we have any tobacco or food, better to share it with them as the German soldiers will confiscate it anyway. Those jumping out the windows are not insane, but very normal people being punished for doing something stupid. Here you are punished for anything, and not just this way. What they are wearing are not at all pajamas, but striped prison uniforms. There is no hope in escaping because the wire has a high electric current running through it. They provide very little food, 250 grams of bread, and ¾ of a liter of what they call soup. As part of punishment someone will remain several days without any food. They are always malnourished.

---

[94] Near Riga, Latvia.

If we are not able to give them anything they will return, as the punishment for talking with a woman is 25 lashes with a whip.

How horrible.

I hastily take out of my suitcase my notes and shove them into my stomach. But I am not able to take it all out. The sentry tells me to go away.

A German woman is organizing us, she is dressed in an SS uniform.[95] Is there also an SS? Apparently yes, because she is screaming and hitting us. After counting us she issues a command for us to run to the barrack and again beats us to get us to hurry. There is a jam at the door. Each is hurrying to squeeze into the barrack to escape her whip. If she notices even the tiniest package or even a purse, she chases that woman back to leave it. She also beats her for this.

The barrack is totally bare: just a ceiling, walls and floor. On the floor are some straw-stuffed mattresses, while in the corner a broom handle. That is it.

The female supervisor hollers at us to lay down. Whoever does not do this at this moment will lose their spot and the broom handle used on them. They beat on the head, shoulders, arms, wherever it falls. When we all lie down she orders us not to move from our spot. The sentries standing at the windows will shoot us at our slightest movement. We must not leave the barrack. Talking is also prohibited.

Placing the broom handle in its place the evil SS walks away. The women call her Elza. Maybe they heard someone call her this, or maybe they gave her this name.

This means I am in a concentration camp. The convicts' uniforms, jumping through the window, and types of even worse punishments, Elza with the broom handle. Deprivation. It is so frightening here! And I am alone. If mama was here. Where is she now? Maybe she is right now standing in the

---

[95] Abbreviation for *Schutzstaffel*, meaning, Protection squadron. A Nazi paramilitary organization.

forest in front of a pit? And during this night, the one who howls at us under the windows is breaking branches in the forest and scaring children! Horrible! Intolerably horrible!

Someone is walking under the windows. No doubt it is a guard. Maybe he is watching us. If the straw mattress did not prick me so much, I would wrap myself in it so the light would not cut into my eyes. Why can I not sleep? So many nights I have not yet slept. Maybe I will dream about mama.

Mama... Rayechka... Ruvik. It was just recently we were together. Ruvik wanted to take his books, "You can read them when you have free time."

A whistle! A long, extended one. I look. At the doors again is that evil Elza. She screams, "*Appell!*" This means, "Roll call." But we do not understand what she is saying and we sit. Elza again grabs the broom handle. We run from the barrack.

It is dark outside, cold. People are also running from other barracks. They are lining up. Elza hits them, curses at them, and then arranges us. One other SS is helping her, a male. Suddenly he straightens in front of an approaching officer. He reports our quantity and accompanies the officer as he counts us himself.

Finishing recounting the officer goes to other barracks.

We look around, searching for our things, but they are nowhere to be seen. In fact we cannot even recognize the place where yesterday we left them. The place is swept clean, and with yellow sand spread over it.

They again chase us into the barrack and again order us to sit on the straw mattresses, not to talk and not to move.

We sit.

Suddenly I feel in my pocket a photograph of my father. (How did it get here?) I look at papa and I felt so bad that I started to sob. He is gone, mama is gone, and here I must alone suffer this torture at this horrible camp. I will never get adjusted to this place. I will not survive.

A woman sitting next to me asks why I am sobbing. I show her the photograph. She only sighs, "Tears will not help."

SS officers suddenly surface at the doors. They order us to assemble. They announce that we must give them all money, watches, rings, in short, all that we possess. For any attempt to hide, bury, or even discard it is capital punishment.

An officer with a box in his hands is walking through the rows. The collection of course is very meager.

Walking away the German officers did not say anything about us sitting. But the threatening broom handle is at the door, like a sentry. We stand.

It is cold. Wind is blowing in through the opened door. So many days I have not eaten.

Elza is again at the door. She thinks it is funny as to why we are still standing. After laughing at us she orders us to stand in twos. She counts ten lines and leads them out. Those standing nearest to the doors inform us that the women were lead into the barrack that is at the end of the block.

Quickly Elza returns, counts another 10 and again leads them out. But the first group did not leave [from their destination]. Is that where the crematorium is located? This means that we were brought here specifically to be eliminated without a trace remaining.

Some women standing closer to the doors ran to the back of the line. Is this possible?

I am in the seventh group of 10. The front rows are decreasing, there are less of them. Soon it will be my turn...

They are now leading me...

Elza is opening the door of this scary barrack. No odor of any sort. Maybe this gas has no odor? Dark shadows. Much clothing is thrown against the walls. Alongside them stands female supervisors. We are also ordered to undress. We are to hold our clothing in our hands and walk up to the supervisors two at a time.

Our hands are shaking, it is difficult to undress. So what am I to do with my notes? I shove them into my armpit and hold it tight to myself. I walk forward. The SS officer searches my clothes. She takes my wool dress that mama told me to wear over my summer dress. I ask her if she will allow me to keep the warm dress, and they can take the summer. But I get a slap in the face and I become silent. Now the SS officer searches my sleeves and pockets if I have hidden anything. She finds papa's photograph. I stretch my hand forward for the supervisor to return it to me, but she shreds the photograph into little pieces and throws them on the floor. I see graying hair on one fragment, and an eye on another. I turn away...

They order us to quickly dress in the clothes they leave for us and to go out through the back door. It appears those who were led out earlier are standing there, while those in the barracks are worried, thinking they will be led to a crematorium.

After they searched us all next was the wretched roll call. Why are they counting us so often? Is it really possible to escape from here?

Finally they release us back to the barrack. To our greatest joy and surprise a kettle of soup and a pile of small bowls are on a table. They order us to stand in one line. As we enter we need to take a bowl and Elza will pour some soup into it. We must eat it quickly and put the bowl back in its place. Even if the bowl is not rinsed it is still used for the next in line. There are no spoons.

The closer to the kettle the more tastier is the odor of the steam coming from it.

Finally it is my turn. Well, the soup is overwhelmingly greasy. It is simply a hot black liquid with these six beans majestically floating in it and which cannot seem to get into my mouth. But nonetheless it is tasty. What is principal is that it is hot. What is sad is that this meal hardly satisfies the appetite. But there is nothing else. I want to eat so badly and more than just this one bowl of soup.

I return the bowl to its place. I watch. A German soldier points his finger at me. Me? Yes, it seems, me. I unpretentiously walk to him and wait for what he wants to say. But he hits me on the cheek, and then on the other, and does it again. He is beating me with his fists. My head is going back and forth. I attempt to shield myself with the bowl, but he grabs it out of my hand and throws it in the corner. And again he is beating me, injuring me. My feet cannot hold me up and I fall. I want to stand but cannot as he is now kicking me with his feet. No matter how I try to turn around the shine of his boots are in front of my eyes. Right in my mouth! I can barely breath. My lips become numb, my tongue swells and hardens. But the German soldier continues to hit me, kick me, but by this time it seems it is not as painful, except that blood is dripping on the floor. No doubt mine...

Finally the German soldiers leave. The women pick me up and help me to my mattress. They advise me to keep my head back so the blood will stop flowing out of my nose. They are so nice, considerate, so much I want to cry. They sigh. What he did to me, an innocent child! Another curses him, while another is trying to figure the reason for him beating me so much. Maybe as I was returning the bowl I got too close to the line and he thought I wanted to get a second portion of soup?

Why are they talking so loud? This is so painful for me, all of me intolerably hurts! At least they can put out the lights! Is my eyebrow lacerated? It also hurts. My front teeth are knocked out.

I barely made it to morning.

Even before daybreak they chased us outside for inspection. (At the concentration camps they inspected us twice a day: early morning and in the evening when all the brigades would return from work.) I can barely stand, my head is howling, my lips and eyes are swollen. If I could just have one swallow of water! They don't give. They order us back into the barrack.

Near noon again they order us in formation. They select 600 women, and then another 400. Those selected were placed in a separate formation, while the rest were herded back into the barrack.

I am in the second group.

From those in the first group they count out 50 and lead them to the edge of the barrack. One of our group was able to read the sign: *Entlausung*,[96] the bathhouse. This is also what they called the gas chambers at the crematoriums.

How much have I experienced and nevertheless the end.

The female supervisor returns and leads away another 50.

And so another 50 each half-hour. But the initial group has not returned.

Now no one remains, the square is empty. Now the turn for our group. Soon they will also lead me.

Unexpectedly we see the entire first group. They are alive! This means we will also live.

The women of this group are climbing into trucks. They wave to us. It became very, very calm.

They lead us into a waiting room. Here are piles of clothing. We can only take our shoes with us and soap and a brush, if someone has this. We need to hold it all in our hands. We need to leave our purses or bags. I was successful to shove some pages of my diary into the stockings of my shoes and under the insoles. Other women also quickly hid a few pages.

They herd us naked into another room. Under the ceiling are several pipes with holes, no doubt a shower. At the door a German soldier in a while smock inspects us, if we hid anything in our shoes or in our hands. I turn the shoes upside down to show there is nothing there. Then I stand to take my turn with the doctor. The "doctor" uses a magnifying glass to examine the cleanliness of my head and orders me to open my

---

[96] delousing or decontamination

mouth. He inserts his finger inside my cheek: Is there something hidden there.

Next with whom to deal is the barber. The scissors are large, and he no doubt is not a barber of any type. The more beautiful the hair the uglier does he cut it to pieces. He shoves the shorn hair and curls into a bag.

Finally they released warmed water from the pipes. It dripped for a new minutes and stopped. We were barely able to get wet, and what made it worse was not having anything to wipe ourselves.

Wet they chased us into an even colder annex. The door to the street was opened and the evil wind was piercing and blowing through cracks in the walls.

Piles of clothes were setting lengthwise along the walls. A female supervisor stood next to each pile. We are supposed to walk along them. From each pile we get one thing: a shirt, pants, dress, coat and scarf. They distribute in order regardless of height or weight. When one girl asked to change her dress because the size was too small for her, the supervisor grabbed the dress and hit the girl with it on the head, threw it down and then laughed at her and said, "Adjust it at the side."

I was able to get stretched and torn and not very clean underclothes. Also a ballroom dress made from black silk with a large décolleté and decorated with red flowers. I was barely able to fit into the coat, it was a child's size. They did not give me any stockings.

Elza at the doors was verifying whether we stole a second set of underclothes or even one more scarf.

Other women of our group stand outside, but I cannot even recognize one of them. If you know a little about someone, at least you can identify them by their clothes, but now this unusual attire has changed them all.

We each get a sheet. I watch, the women coil it around their necks. Taking their example I do the same.

An unfamiliar girl walks up to me and asks about changing coats, because hers is especially big for her. I am very glad. Finally I can freely breath, not fearing that I will tear the seams. Now my sole problem is the dress, it is so narrow that I can barely take a step in it. But the women comfort me, it will no be so cold for my feet. But my back is bare.

Our clothes are labeled; on the chest and back are large circles or crosses made with an oil-based paint.

After all of us bathed they herded us into trucks. There are two guards in each. They take us. It is dark. We drive out of the forest and turn onto the highway.

This time the route was not long. We entered some kind of large yard. It is surrounded by a high rock wall, over it are several rows of barb wire and lights. No barracks. Only one immense building. At the end of the yard is a canopy with lamps swinging at its corners. Pleasant odors are emanating from it. Maybe this is the kitchen and they will give us some soup. A German in civilian clothes arranges us. He is wearing a dark semi-military suit and hat that almost appears like an inmate's. He counts us and orders us not to move from this spot, but then he walks away. Timidly we look about, several men are walking toward us. We find out from one of them that this camp is named Strasdenhof[97] and is located in an area of Riga called Jugla. This is a new camp. There are only 65 men here so far from the Riga ghetto. There are no women, we are the first. We will live in this large building. This was a former factory. The men's section is on the first floor, ours will be on the fourth. They do not know where we will work. They are still making arrangements. The work will be very difficult, and worse because we are so hungry. The camp elder or supervisor is also German, his name is Hans. He is also an inmate. He has been sitting in various camps now for eight years. It is not known why. He has an assistant, young Hans. The commander

---

[97] also called Riga-Strasdenhof or Shtraznov

of the camp is an SS officer, an *unterscharführer*,[98] he is a terrifying sadist.

Suddenly the men scattered, they noticed the approaching *unterscharführer*. He again counted us and walked away. Soon Hans ordered blankets to be brought to us and started to distribute them. But not for me, instead of a blanket I got a large peasant shawl. But how will it keep me warm?

Then they served us cold soup and chased us to the fourth floor. This is our section. It is very much like a dormitory. Bunk beds three high made of wood boards were built inside of it. There are five compartments on this floor. Thirty-six women are assigned to sleep in each compartment; 18 on one side and 18 on the other. Bags to be used as straw-mattresses are thrown on the bunk beds and smaller bags for pillows.

Hans ordered each of us to occupy a place. One compartment was supposed to remain empty, more women will be brought here. We will fill the mattresses tomorrow after work. Right now we must lay down. In the morning, after hearing the signal, we must immediately rise and get outside to wash.

One neighbor woman advised us to remove several strands from the rope in the bag and tie them together to use to secure our dresses. Otherwise we will not be able to work. Smart woman.

"Stand!" Hans is shouting.

Why? Didn't we just lie down? And outside it is totally dark.

Hans is very mean. Maybe it is actually morning? We grab our sheet and throw them down along the staircase. Hans goes insane as a result of this. He shouts, We have overslept so we have to run to inspection unwashed.

The men are already standing in formation, but we are still figuring what to do. Finally Hans shouts, *"Stillstand!"*, meaning "Stand still!" and runs with his report to the *unterscharführer*. He counts us and leaves.

---

[98] junior squad leader of the SS

Now Hans is out of control. There needs to be exemplary order and discipline in the camp. Who violates this will be severely punished. He will no longer run to waken us, we need to attend to the signal – some bangs on metal. Once hearing the first signal we must at that very moment jump out of bed, fold our bunk, and run to wash (and for the meanwhile to the stream flowing alongside the camp). After the second signal we must momentarily assemble for inspection.

He still led us to wash. It is dark, a piercing wind is blowing, rain is pouring, my hands are getting numb from the cold water, but we need to wash, otherwise we will fall behind.

It starts to light. We are again assembled. The *unterscharführer* arrives with his assistants and convoy guards. They divide us into groups and lead us away.

The first group walks forward, while we quickly turn to the right. We arrive at the site. Men from our camp are already working here, they were brought here right after inspection.

They order me to carry rocks. The men are paving the road between barracks under construction. Other women are hauling rocks from the ravine in wheeled carts,[99] while we need to carry them to the stonemasons. The convoy guards and supervisors not for a minute take their eyes off of us. The wheeled carts need to be full, and four of us need to push them running. We also need to run when we deliver rocks, the men are responsible to quickly arrange them. All needs to be done quickly and efficiently, otherwise they will shoot us.

The rocks are horribly heavy. For two persons to carry one rock is not permitted. We cannot roll it either. Talking during work is prohibited. Only once a day is a person allowed to take care of natural needs, and even then you need to wait until several persons are together. A guard will not take a person by himself.

As though deliberately the rain does not stop pouring.

---

[99] The word can also refer to a small cart on rails or a wheelbarrow.

I have cut my fingers, they are bleeding. They are blue, swollen and horrible to look at.

Finally the whistle for lunch. We are quickly arranged and led to the camp. Those sanding first immediately get soup, but we need to wait until they drink theirs and free their bowls. We hurry them, afraid we may not get any.

So it happened. I only drank a few swallows, and the guard was already chasing us to work. He grabbed the bowl out of my hand, the soup spilled and I, now even hungrier, was supposed to stand in formation.

Again I haul rocks. Now they seem to be heavier. And the rain more intolerable. One rock slipped out of my hands and right on my foot.

I barely made it to evening. Returning to camp we each received a piece of bread and some dirty water they called coffee. I swallowed all of it right there in the yard. I had no patience to wait until I walked up to the fourth floor.

Once I caught on to carrying rocks they assigned me to break them into small pieces. I of course could not. I hit with the hammer, but the rock is still one piece. I hit it harder but a fragment flew off and it went right into my face. It is bleeding and hurts, I am afraid to injure my eyes. But the guard is shouting at me to hurry. One man offers to teach me, but the guard refuses him, I need to learn on my own. I close my eyes, I cry from the pain and offense and continue to hammer.

I ask everybody, if anyone finds a piece of a pencil, save it for me. I need to urgently restore the lost notes from the ghetto. I am so glad mama ordered me to learn by memory what I wrote. But I had many notes and I am afraid that I could forget. All day breaking rocks, I remember, I repeat. But I cannot stop, I will forget, this is why it is so important for me to inscribe on my mind the present experience here.

I got a pencil! One of the men "stopped" me (he threw it when the guard was not watching). Paper is not a problem.

There are empty bags all over that held cement and which we use to wrap our feet (they still did not give us stockings). It is warm for our feet and in this manner we can bring paper into the camp without any risk.

I continue to break rocks. My face is somewhat healed, the fragments are not flying at me so often, I have learned. But the work is nonetheless still hard, and it is cold and wet. We have not seen one person from the outside; we know nothing about the front, and it is difficult to guess anything based on the German soldiers' moods.

I miss mama very much. Can it really be that she is no longer? Did they also kill the children? One woman told me that the fascists do horrible experiments: they pull off the skin. They drain the blood out of the children. They draw it out of the veins until the child drops dead. Unbelievable, horrible, this cannot be! Did they actually torture Ruvik this way? No way can I escape from this nightmare, it revolves within me, that Ruvik is sitting on some shelf with a large needle stuck in his hand and is turning pale, weakening, dying.

The beasts! And we need to work for them. Maybe all of us can get together and agree to throw all these rocks right at them, then they can shoot us. At least we will know why.

When imagining becomes intolerably difficult, I try to recollect the past... I loved to sit home in such good weather. If papa did not have any visitors, I would slither into his office, whirl in his chair and read a book. How nice it was!

I hear the angry shout of a convoy guard. The office and warmth disappear. Only the camp remains, the rocks, the rain.

Now I am doing a different work – I push wheeled carts. We move rocks and sand. We need to push full wheeled carts uphill, and run downhill with them.

It is difficult to haul them. No way can I let one go, otherwise the wheeled cart will run down the hill and kill not only us but those but those dragging theirs behind us. It is difficult to get it to the top of the hill, we need to load the wheeled cart, move it to some rails, and holding it tight, run up the hill. What makes it more difficult is that an empty wagon wants to move fast down the hill, we barely keep up with it from behind but cannot let it go, otherwise it will kill someone. One was already crushed. He was a professor from Riga University. Was...

It is already November. It is getting colder each day. My coat and shoes are sopping wet. They still do not give us stockings. The paper wrapping does not help. What has to be the worst is having to put on wet clothes every morning, the barrack is not heated, during the night my clothes do not dry.

It is somewhat better for those who work in the factory: it is dry and warm there. Other than this they teach them traditional Latvian weaving, which acquires bread for them.

Day before yesterday luck smiled on me; I found a needle! A genuine, whole needle! Although I got a kick from a guard for this, that I dared bend down to the floor, but no big deal, it was worth it for the needle. At least I will get my dress to fit. The woman on the next bunk will teach me. Among other things, she is my namesake: Masha. She is somewhat older than me, very intelligent and practical, but with a dry character. She will not acknowledge someone in a bad mood or melancholy. Now she has no choice when someone complains.

I do not just sleep next to her but sit at the same table. These tables set lengthwise along the walls, each holding 20 women. The female supervisor gets enough bread for everyone. She distributes the crust on top equally, and everyone wants a piece since it is solid and you can chew on it longer.

Finally my dress looks like something. True it is not straight at the bottom, as I have no scissors and I had to tear it using my hands and hem it using white thread, and I was able to get the back and neck covered.

But now a new problem: my shoes are torn apart, they almost fall off my feet. The top is in half, the sole is worn

through, my toes stick out. I am afraid of losing them. They
barely held together while I was still at the ghetto, but now
they are wet from rain and shredded by the rocks, they are
totally ruined.

Masha works at the factory. She brings me thread, some of
them are used to weave rope and tie soles onto shoes. But when
the thread gets wet it tears and my shoe again opens. What
will happen during winter? I cannot walk barefooted in the
snow.

Masha advises me to ask Hans about it. If there are clothes
in the storage, no doubt there are also shoes. But I do not dare,
better for me to tolerate a while longer.

Sunday. We work only to 3 o'clock and return to the camp while
it is still light. The camp looks unusual, not at all what it looks
like in the dark. An inscription gloomily hangs in the daylight,
"You do not live to work, you work to live." And the fence now
seems to be much higher, more frightening.

But this is not important. What is now more important is
Hans' latest innovation. Summoning the block supervisor and
several girls he informs them that every Sunday in the
evening, they must perform a concert, or else they will become
his *speziell Freunde*. But the meaning of this expression we did
not figure soon enough. He would tend to find more faults in
the "special friends," punish them more frequently, send them
to harder work, and leave them without bread.

Masha suggested I write some poetry. About what? While in
school I would compose verses about spring, nature, the moon
and stars. Once the teacher brought a vinyl record of
Beethoven's *Sixth Symphony*. Listening to it at my lessons I
wrote my impression of it in verse. Almost a complete notebook.
The teacher even liked it and memorized some of it. But what
can I write about here?

Masha orders me to write about us. Verses? I cannot
imagine this. It is one thing to describe facts, events, another

are verses. What kind of poetry can be composed while under such circumstances.

Yesterday after inspection Hans asked whether the program for the concert was ready. The supervisor of the block answered in a regimented manner, "*Jawohl,*" meaning, "Certainly." (If she would have said the truth she would have been beaten.)

My legs are falling out from under me, tomorrow the concert must be performed and I did not yet write even one line. All day, pushing the wheeled cart, I attempted to express something of myself. But the more I tried the less it happened.

In the evening I confessed to Masha that I had written nothing. No matter how hard I try my mind retains only one thing: I am sad, I miss my mother, the work is intolerably difficult, it is cold and I so much want to eat.

Masha did not like my excuses. She responded maliciously and said that this is exactly what I need to write about.

No, she does not understand me. But she is not mama who would listen to all I would say, have empathy, and advise me on what to write. Maybe about the greasy soup, about the tied and mended shoes, or my legs turning blue from the cold

Certain thoughts flashed in my head. I ran to the toilet where there are less people, and there in the corner on the window sill I started to write. But this was not in verse.

Today in the second and vacant block several tables were moved together. This became the stage. On one side of the hall the men would stand, on the other the women. The concert is already starting and I am correcting and emending my "creation." Now Masha is a bit more joyful. She boasted that someone gave me a pair of shoes and ordered me not to get excited over it.

When my presentation was announced I climbed on the tables. I thought I should make some reference as in school, an introduction. I sat, but very clumsily it seems, and no one, no doubt, understood what this was supposed to mean.

It was with my hoarse voice that I started to read my verbal newspaper, *The Women's Express*. I read as though an operator was reading various telegraphic messages, that a truckload of wool stockings was sent to us. But not shoes yet because people walk here barefooted. The potatoes for our soup are not yet dug up, there are more important matters to tend to. And so forth.

Initially my feet shook, but quickly I felt that people were sighing approvingly and even smiling, I became calm. I got down from the table completely calm.

Following me a group of women sang *Evening Bells*. One girl from Riga played a polka on her comb, while another sang a very sad love song.

After the concert they gave to us, the participants, half a bowl of cold soup. Masha ordered me to take advantage of Hans' good mood and ask for a pair of shoes. But I could not get myself to do it. She went out of control, telling me that with such a character I will lose out and she went herself. Hans told her that this was a concentration camp, and so they do not wear shoes, but wooden boots. Soon some will be brought for the men and then maybe he will get a pair for me.

What happened yesterday I will probably never forget.

In the morning after when we lined up in our brigades for inspection, Hans selected 50 women out of our brigade and me among them, and ordered us to join another brigade that was going to work at the factory *Uglas Manufactura*.[100]

Finally my sufferings ended! No more will I have to push these horrible wheeled carts and get soaked in the rain.

We walk along an unfamiliar road. The new environment is alien to me: all is unfamiliar, unknown, not knowing what

---

[100] Located in northeast Riga.

awaits me. But what I am more afraid of is that I cannot imagine myself having to weave.

They brought us to the factory. Those who started here from the first day went to their workstations, boldly moving along the narrow passages, not fearing the large or small carts. While we, the new workers, packed ourselves into this corner so not to interfere with anybody.

Noise. Wheels are spinning, hitting, rattling. The head of our brigade with this Latvian man, obviously the foreman, leads us along one passage to this workstation and orders us to learn to do this from the Latvian weavers.

I watch but understand none of it. The wheels rotate, these rods with belts push the gears and cause a series of needles to go up and down, and again go up and down. The thread is drawn through the needles and the material flows along.

I look at the other women, what they are doing. As with myself some are just watching, while someone is explaining the procedure to others. Finally my female instructor guesses that I do not understand and shows me how the woven bags are weaved. Once I watched how she did it then I understood, but when I took the thread in my calloused hands the thread slipped out and no way was I able to succeed to make this bag.

The rest of the day this Latvian woman did not show me how to do anything else, I was supposed to learn on my own to quickly weave these bags. Time stretched forever, worse than at the site (but so it is at a new place), but not so bad as it was warm. So at evening when I went into the street it seemed to me very cold. On the way back to the camp I trudged in a daze: my head ached and the noise and rattle echoed in it. I did not even want to eat much, although I had nothing in my mouth since the day before. Now in general we eat twice a day, we have soup at lunch, and bread with what they call coffee in the evening. Few people have the moral strength to divide their morsel of bread in half and save it for morning. We all know we need to really do this, and we all have tried to do this many times, but it never happens. It is worth it for me to leave at least the smallest crumb, but during the night I awake and do not fall asleep again until I pull it out from under my straw mattress and eat it. I am comforted only that it will be morning soon, and I would have eaten it anyway.

Today I am also planning to save some, but today we just had one meal and all they served was soup and bread. But it was so tasty that I did not even notice that I ate it all.

I still have this howling in my head. I barely awaited the signal to allow us to sleep.

I woke up because someone was intently shaking me. It seems to still be night, but a light was on in the barrack, but no one at all in the other bunk beds. The supervisor of my table orders me to quickly rise. Behind her back stands Hans.

I climb out. What has happened? The supervisor throws a coat on my shoulders and leads me to the table. Everyone else is already sitting at their places. When I get near the *unterscharführer* hit me so hard on the face that my eyeballs shook. He was completely out of control and did not allow me to catch my breath. I am trying to stand on my feet, so he would not kick me if I fall.

Finally he got tired of hitting me and let me go. He ordered me to stand on my knees the entire night.

Hans whistled for all to lay down, but he took me to the staircase and ordered me to stand on my knees at the feet of the sentry. He was ordered to watch over me so I do not attempt to stand and so no one gives me any shoes.

How can I endure this? It is cold. My knees are bleeding and hurt. The sentry does not allow me to make a move and time stretches so intolerably slow.

I can barely keep myself together. It seems I am ready to collapse at any moment. But the sentry hits me with his rifle butt and I again straighten.

The sentries change. This means only two hours remain. It is so far from morning and there is no way I will survive. But when I sleep it seems the night passes so fast.

They pick me up in the morning, I cannot straighten my legs. They order me to inspection, I could not walk, I keep falling.

Now I found out the reason for my punishment. It appears that at night the insane Hans flew in the barrack and whistled. He ordered everyone to get in formation in the passages between the bunk beds. Then the *unterscharführer* ran in. Both started to deliriously count the lines. Yes, they were one short. The sentry at the gates suggested that one person escaped through a sewer pipe. They counted again. Not enough. They ordered everyone to get arranged in their brigades, they needed to determine who escaped. But fortunately today the number to work at the factory increase and the brigadier did not yet know everybody. Then they ordered everyone to sit at their tables, 20 at each.

I was not there. The tables' supervisor instinctively looked into the bunks. It was solely my bare foot that was sticking out from under my shawl in the far corner.

Hans reminded me. Immediately after the morning inspection he shouted, "The one who slept through the night inspection, three steps forward!" I shook, will he again beat me? I barely stood. Then I walked forward. Hans surveyed me, frowned and asked where I worked. Finding out that it was at the factory, he ordered me to return to the site.

The warm life ended, but only for one day. Still my coat did not have time to dry. Again I was soaked from the rain, and I trampled in the mud almost barefooted.

They brought new people. They were from Germany. They quickly assigned one of them to be the supervisor of our barrack, and the person she replaced was sent to the site.

Some of the new arrivals were assigned to our barrack, the remaining in the second.

They brought another load of persons – these from the Riga ghetto. Also through Kaiserwald and also half-naked. But the children were not removed or even the aged. They were not separated. How nice for them!

I ask if any of them knows my aunt in Riga.[101] Sadly I still know nothing of what occurred to her. I hope she is found!

The first snow fell. Finally they issued us stockings. True they are not much like real stockings. They are socks, and men's for the most part, in different colors, and pieces of women's stockings are sewn over them as patches or else they are just rags. But I need to be happy at least to wear these in December.

I returned to the factory. They say Masha convinced the brigadier to talk to Hans on my behalf. I am assigned to the same Latvian woman. I start again with the bags.

Now I am able to stop the machine and release the device and change thread when the spool is empty and place another in the device.

I am not as cold, but hunger does bother me.

They brought a truck load of wooden shoes. When they were unloaded I took the chance of walking up to Hans. He ordered someone to show me the shoes. Then he ordered the person who handles distribution of clothing to give me a pair of boots and to take my shoes. It was a pity to have to give them up, it was the last of the items that I brought from home. But nothing I could do as they were falling to pieces.

In the clothing storage they did not even ask me my size. They just grabbed the first pair they could and threw it to me. These boots were too large, but to ask for another pair was considered insolent. I will shove paper into it to keep my feet

---

[101] Pesya Rolnick, 1917-1942/43. The sister of Masha's father.

from sliding and so will wear them. This "wealth" is heavier than pieces of wood tied together with oilcloth. It was also recorded: "*Haftling* #5007 received one pair of wooden boots." I was inmate #5007. Family and personal names do not exist here, you are just a number. I adjusted myself to it and answer when called by this number. At the factory this number is sewn on my work smock. (I already work independently.) After every 50 meters of cloth there is a blue spot. At this spot I need to cut the woven fabric and at both ends I need to imprint my number and pass it along. Passing it along I, as with others, mentally wish that the fascists will use this material for bandages.

Initially, after finally learning how to independently work, I strove hard and almost each day manufactured 50 meters of cloth. Now they taught me how to sabotage: just unscrew some gear a little bit or cut the cloth, and the device will jam. I call the foreman, he digs around, fixes it, and then records on a card how many hours the machine was down.

Each day it seems that somebody's machine breaks down, and for a different reason.

It seems there is nothing else in the world as far as I am presently concerned apart from the camp, work, hunger and cold.

At this time in the past the weather should already be thawing, but right now as though on purpose, the frost is ruthless day to day. My jacket is for the summer, my dress is silk and without sleeves. The frost penetrates right through while I walk to work and back. My knees turn blue and hurt as if burning inside. By the time we return to the camp and enter our barrack they are calling us for inspection.

We get stiff while standing. The *unterscharführer* is deliberately in no hurry to go outside, and so we need to stand in the frost and not make a move.

But if someone should suddenly ignore him in his presence during counting, or makes some motion, as punishment he will required us to stand in freezing weather to midnight.

This week I am working on the night shift. Its sole advantage is that it is possible to escape this horrible punishment of standing in the frost. But in general the night shift is more difficult: as morning approaches you want to sleep so bad, the bright light of the factory cuts into your eyes, and your stomach groans from hunger. In the morning we are half-alive and frozen and so return to the camp, the cold does not allow us to sleep. The wind blows and carries snow into the empty barrack through cracks in the frozen windows. At night when many people are sleeping it is a little warmer. But Hans does not allow two per bunk to share blankets and keep each other warm; he says we need to temper ourselves. On purpose he comes to inspect us to see how we are sleeping. If he notices someone under two blankets he chases that person naked outside.

Recently, more often does it seem to me that I cannot endure any more of this. My heart is ready to fail on me. But it does not fail and the pain subsides, and then back to the old routine: I rise, I sleep, I follow the whistle.

I spoke with one woman from Riga who knew my aunt and uncle when they were residing in Riga before the war. It is sad both are already in the ground. My uncle was shot during the initial days [of the occupation], while my aunt and her two children were confined in the Riga ghetto. She starved there since she could not leave for work, as there was no place to leave the children. Eventually she and both her children were taken from there and shot.

Yesterday's terror is horrifying for me to recollect but I cannot forget it.

In the evening when those working at the site returned from work, they were intensely searched at the entrance: the convoy guard informed the sentries that he saw a passer-by give one of the inmates a piece of bread. It was found on two men, each had half. The incident was reported to the *unterscharführer* during evening inspection.

So the inspection ended. Instead of the brigades dispersing the *unterscharführer* ordered both criminals to step forward, stand in line and undress. They were hesitant – snow and cold. But after a few whips they were submissive. We were not allowed to turn away. We had to watch this lesson they were to impose on them for the future. This was not all.

They brought two buckets of warm water from the kitchen and poured it over their heads. The poor souls are shivering, their teeth are shattering, their underclothes are sticking to them, steam is emanating from them, but it did not matter. The soldiers bring two more buckets of warm water. They are again poured over the heads of the poor souls. They start to jump, while the soldiers and the *unterscharführer* are laughing at them.

The exercise is repeated every 20 minutes. Both can barely stand on their feet. They no longer look like humans: the bald head of the older one is covered with a thin sheet of ice, while the hair of the younger, which he is tearing and mangling in his suffering, are freezing together like icicles. Their underclothes are totally frozen and their feet are dead white. The guards are rolling over with laughter. They think this "Christmas decoration" is funny. They are advising each other as to how to pour the next bucket of water on them. "Into his pants," shouted one, "Dump it on his head," hollered another.

The tortured couple are attempting to turn around and run, but they are caught just like escaping animals and returned to their spot. And if they move to have some of the water splash away from them, the water wasted, then another whole bucket is brought. The poor souls only raise one foot at a time so not to freeze to the snow on the ground.

They will not endure this! They will go insane! What are they doing to them!

Finally the German soldiers get tired. They order us to disperse. Hans gives a order for these two not to be released from work, even if the temperature is 40 degrees below freezing.

The older one died today. He fell near his wheeled cart and did not get up. The second worked although barely able to stay on his feet, delirious from fever. When the guards were not watching friends attempted to help him somehow finish all his work, otherwise he will not escape being shot.

Hans then devised a new means of mockery: "ventilation of the lungs."

On Sunday the factories are closed, this is why those who work at the factories are sent to the site. This would not be so bad if these were to replace the site workers for a day, to allow them the day off to get warm. But since Hans does not allow a day off, he compels them "to ventilate their lungs." From early morning they must march through the camp and sing. Hans especially likes this one special song that he composed particularly for us: "We were masters of the world, now we are the lice of the world."

The worse the freezing weather the longer that Hans compels us to march.

Today one woman told me not to write any more funny stories. What am I laughing at? At our miseries?

I complained to Masha. She gave me the riot act: I do not need to try to please everyone, because tomorrow someone might say the complete opposite. I need to think on my own, what comes into my head. To write is necessary. If my *Strasdenhof hymn*[102] is sung by the entire camp, this means the majority like this song. This is primary.

I guess she was right.

---

[102] Can be accessed at https://collections.ushmm.org

The SS agents conceived a new punishment.

Maybe it is not so much a punishment as plainly more of a practical stunt. It will soon be spring and to hold us in freezing weather seems to have lost their interest.

After inspection Hans ordered us to stand in formation and to have about a meter between the rows. They he ordered us to squat and jump. Initially we did not understand what he wanted us to do, but Hans hollered so loud that, even not understanding him, we started to jump.

My legs barely hold me up. I can hardly breath. And Hans is walking between the rows, hitting us with his whip and shouting for us to not malinger. We cannot sit, we need to jump, jump like frogs.

My heart is rapidly beating, I am getting tired! Let me just rest for a minute. My side aches! I hurt all over, I cannot do this any longer! But Hans does not turn his eyes away.

One girl fainted and fell. Soon the same will happen to me. Hans does not allow us to get near the girl lying on the ground who fainted. All need to jump. Another girl falls. She motions for help, indicating that she cannot talk anymore. Someone cries in horror, "She is unconscious!"

Finally Hans also gets tired of it. He releases us. He does not allow us to pick up the girls who are unconscious. "They are feigning this. They will get up themselves." But if they are unconscious this means they are weak and cannot work, we need to record their number. Women grab the poor souls and drag them further from Hans. They are in no condition to straighten on their own. Almost on all fours we pull our friends as they are still not totally conscious. But only as far as the staircase. We cannot carry them upstairs. We sit on the slab floor and give them mouth to mouth respiration. Some women attempt climbing the stairs, but they stop to sit after just a few difficult steps. I am still out of breath, I cannot seem to get back to normal breathing. I ask one woman to help me lean against the handrail, maybe holding on to it I might make it to the top. But what for? I can hardly talk. The harder I try the harder it is to say something.

I decide to not talk anymore.

I creep upwards. I would lie down but not before the signal. I collapse on the bench at the table, I put my head on my hands and lie there. But now it is harder for me to breath, I have to straighten. I see these half-dead and hardly breathing humans dragging themselves in through the door.

Suddenly Hans surfaces at the doors. He surveys us, he is perplexed and quiet, not knowing what to say. "Today is Sunday, a day off of work, you need to sing."

We are silent.

"Sing," he hollers maliciously. "Or you will jump."

One started to sing with her shivering voice, then another woman squeaked. A few other hoarse voices supported them. I tried to also. My mouth opens but salty tears flow into it.

We just found out why day before yesterday they forced us to jump. Someone told the German soldiers about "conversations of mutiny" we were supposedly having.

Who could have said this? Who is trying to cater to them? Everyone is suspicious of "that corner," meaning those who were brought from Germany. But how can we know the truth? How to find the female traitor?

The girls decided to investigate all those newly arrived. In the presence of just one of them somebody will say something about the *unterscharführer* or Hans. If they do not punish us for this, then she was not the betrayer. Then go to another. So to investigate all until the genuine traitor is determined.

They will not include me with the investigators, I could fail and I have already suffered far more than others: I have teeth knocked out and spent the entire night on my knees. And just now am I starting to talk normally after the jumping.

But I nevertheless wrote a song about it. I call it *Sport*. I do not want them to think their stunts are so horrifying and we girls cannot endure it. It is more of an inconvenience to us.

This morning during inspection Hans announced that someone in our barrack misplaced a pair of shoes. One woman came to ask him for boots, because she could not go barefooted to work. Who stole these shoes?

Silence...

Hans was furious. If the shoes are not found by evening he will figure a means to punish us. There must not be theft in the camp.

On exiting to work everyone was carefully searched. Of course, the shoes were not found.

This theft did not provide calm the entire day. Who could have taken them? And for what reason? The thief could not wear them, or hide them, the only place being the straw mattress, and the German soldiers search here regularly. Or take them out, since they are old and torn and nothing to get for them if you sell them. Some women were convinced that this theft was a provocation, or that the woman herself plainly hid them to get another pair of boots.

Before evening inspection I proposed that we remove our stockings, no doubt we would have to jump, and what they call stockings will not hold out. But no one was in a hurry to follow my example, it was too cold.

After inspection Hans announced that he will show us what it means to steal. He ordered us to get arranged so to jump.

"Didn't I say this?" I whispered to Masha and laughed. Hans noticed this and order me to approach him.

I froze. He drug me out of formation and started to hit me, again on the head. All turned black as I lost my vision. As from a distance I interpreted the sound he was making to mean that he was ordering me to jump *solieren*, to jump solo in front of everyone.

We are all jumping, I am in front of them and they are opposite me. And Hans as usual is running between the rows with foam at his mouth and still staring at me. "You know how to laugh, you know how to jump."

I can hardly breathe. My strength was exhausted. I could not even stop for a second to catch my breath. It seems I am no longer jumping, but that my legs, numb and painful, are mechanical lifting me like a spring, and then releasing me, raising me from the ground and releasing me.

I almost do not remember when he dispersed us and how Masha pulled me, hardly alive, up the stairs. Then Hans it seems ordered us to sing, but we were all quiet. Walking away he threatened us, that tomorrow we will again jump.

Masha wrote a poem about the camp. As far as I was concerned, nothing could be comparable to this. I am only able to laugh at my miseries. But her poem was serious. She inserted profound anguish into it, but it did not contain hopelessness. At the end of it she said directly that the ice will begin to break, the walls will collapse, and then people will fall over each other liberated from these fetters!

Yesterday they was an *aktion*... There is one beginning here...

During the evening inspection many security guards flooded the yard. Initially we did not turn our attention to them, but after noticing that they were surrounding us, and others were entering the barracks, we became afraid.

What is going to happen?

The inspection went as always. Hans counted. The stokers ran from the boiler room and the bakers from the kitchen (they were allowed to run at the last moment), then the *unterscharführer* came. All was the usual.

But nonetheless something was going on...

What are the security guards doing in the barracks? A search? And I have my diary in my mattress. Masha told me a while back to bury it. Why did I postpone it? Now they will find it...

Why are they surrounding us? To see who rushes there because something is hidden in the straw in their mattress? Maybe. But this is more than just a search. Too much security.

The *unterscharführer* has already counted us, but the commanders are not allowing us to disperse. They only release the bakers and stokers.

Out of the second barrack the soldiers are leading two elderly Riga woman. They were sick and so did not show at the inspection. (Hans mentioned in his report that two were sick.) They are being taken to these black covered trucks. We did not even notice when they drove in. Other soldiers were taking away children from women who were standing at the end of the formation. At first glance no one understood anything, but suddenly this horrifying cry arose. The mothers threw themselves at the truck, not wanting to give up their children; they are crying, weeping, cursing. One is begging the security guard to allow her to go together with her son. Another falls on the ground and clenches the soldier's leg so he could not carry away her child. But the soldier kicks her in the face with his boot and walks away with this child in his arms, who is wailing due to all the shouting. The young woman tries with all her strength to retrieve her child, she bites the soldier, but two others grab her, break her arms and drag her away to the side. She helplessly struggles in their arms, shaking her head, screaming, but she cannot wrestle away from them.

One mother is herself taking her daughter to the truck. The German soldier grabs the child and wants to throw her into the truck, but the girl embraces him by the neck and will not let go. The mother grabs her head and wallows on the ground as though knocked down. The German soldier steps over her and shoves the girl into a truck.

They are leading away the aged. The mothers throw themselves at them asking them to watch over their children, telling them their names, pointing at which truck they are in.

The black sides of the trucks indicate something ominous to occur and they drive away. The mothers remain behind. They scream, wail, sob, tear the hair from their heads. Some faint and we cannot seem to get them conscious. They lie on the ground, their hands convulsing, grabbing clods of dirt from the tire tracks.

It is now spring.

The girls were counted. That Saturday, during the *aktion* affecting the children, they hauled 60 sacrifices: 41 children and 19 ages men and women.

We are again jumping. Masha was whispering to me the entire time to teach me how to breathe: inhale, hold my breath, exhale and jump rhythmically, jumping during exhale. And when the *unterscharführer* turns away, only raise your shoulders, imitating jumps.

When it became dark the *unterscharführer* released us. The effect was not the same in the dark. Then he ordered no bread to be given to our barrack. As we were walking away he threatened us, "If even one time you will speak uncomplimentary about German authority, you will be shot without warning, not only the one saying this, but also those who listened and those who did not tell her to stop."

This is the reason we jumped so much!

It appears that Rosa was the traitor. The girls want to beat her up, but I said that we need to think of another punishment, but what I don't know yet. Maybe to ignore her, not to talk to her. The girls would not accept this; it was too objective. At least to kick her in the side and no less!

I was assigned to be the guard at the doors; if the sentry came I was to motion to them.

At night, as we discussed the manner to execute this, they awoke me and barefooted (boots will give us away) we went to our stations. Others climbed on the highest bunk, over the one where Rosa slept (she was in the middle). One girl changed her voice and woke her telling her that a girl was sick. (Rosa was a nurse before the war.) As soon as Rosa was wide awake a blanket was thrown over her from above. The girls jumped, grabbed her as she was fighting from under the blanket, and started to beat her. They beat her with all their strength, but so quietly, that I almost heard nothing at my post, although I knew what was occurring.

I laid down but could not fall asleep for a long while. What will happen if she complains? True, she does not know who it was. But this does not mean anything as all will be punished. Maybe it was not really necessary to beat her? Maybe a threat on the first occasion would have been enough.

Today Rosa is walking about remorseful and with swollen eyes, not looking at anybody. But it is obvious that she is afraid to complain.

A few days ago Masha told me that the women of our table decided to celebrate May First. Getting our share of bread we would not swallow it as usual, immediately, but would all sit together at the table. Someone promised to somehow get a newspaper and tell us what it said. Of course, the fascist newspapers have little truth available, but at least we will hear what cities they have abandoned due to "strategic reasons" or "aligning the front."

And so yesterday we relocated three tables (many decided to join us) and we sat. Liza was telling the news regarding the front. We toss around our guess as to when the Red Army could arrive. We eat our bread slowly, in small pieces. We had never felt this good since arriving and while talking about liberation.

Suddenly I froze, the *unterscharführer* was at the door! And Liza for some reason said "Greetings," instead of the assigned,

"*Achtung.*" He gave this impression as though he did not notice. I said in my hoarse voice, "Many happy years," and then I noticed that Masha was singing a Polish tune, *A Hundred Years*. Then when the *unterscharführer* gave an indication that he ascertained what we were saying, Liza shouted, "*Achtung.*" We jumped from our places and got in line and waited. What will occur now?

The *unterscharführer* looked at us, wondering what we were up to, and asked why we were gathered. Without a blink Liza answers that we were commemorating the supervisor's birthday. The *unterscharführer* cautiously looked at us again and left.

And if Liza did not catch on to stretch the song? Masha laughs at my naivety; this was decided ahead of time.

On Sunday those of us from the factory, as always, worked at the site. As soon as the convoy guard would turn away, I would raise my head and look at the blossoming lilacs on the other side of the road. It seems that the wind was deliberately bending the stems in our directions for the aroma to blow toward us.

When we retuned to the camp, the ones who remained there were "ventilating their lungs," marching with the same song. It was a typical Sunday picture. But suddenly Hans announced that after dinner no one is to leave the barracks: a commission of doctors is coming to inspect our health.

This is strange. We are very thin, almost like skeletons, and what is worse than this, due to the poor food and emotional distress we have abscesses on our body, and especially on our hands and feet. They leak puss and do not heal. Our sole manner of treatment is that in the mornings and evenings we place a cloth soaked in cold water over them. We have become so accustomed to these sores that it is as though we have had them all our life. So what will happen when these German doctors see them?

What to do? Where to hide? Maybe not to show myself and sit in the toilet the entire time? But what if they look there? I ask Masha for her advice. So she replies that there is no need to ask advice in such situations because every person can become the master of their life only on their own. So what a time to philosophize! So what is she going to do? She will go, although her feet are filled with abscesses. But some women whose body is filled with abscesses need to be hidden.

The *unterscharführer* decided on my behalf: he ordered the soldiers to search all corners and until the search is completed, no one is to be allowed into the toilet.

We were ordered to strip naked and then slowly one by one walk past the commission.

The initial group already passed. The most emaciated, with continuous sores, they stopped and asked for their number and would record it in their notebooks.

Soon it will be my turn. I stand together with others, I shake; it is cold and scary. My skin is already blue. I am naked as a jaybird. My buttocks ache. I stand the entire time, my hair is pulled uncomfortably down from my head so it covers the soars on my neck. My hand hurts as it is firmly pressed to my side, it hides the sores under my arms. As long as they do not ask me to raise my hand!

The line moves so slowly...

I am getting close. How do I cope with my legs they do not look bent? I need to be calm so they do not notice that I am afraid. I need to breathe deeply to get as much air in and maybe then I will not look so skinny. If only they release me, I hope they do not stop me.

They call me! No, not me, I am next.

I walk by. I glance at them inconspicuously. The woman behind me stands in front of the commission. The German officer tells her to turn around. He inspects her. He says something to the second SS agent. The woman looks at them with an inquisitive expression. But this does not help. They ask for her number. They record it... The line moves forward.

After examining all the residents of our block of barracks, the commission moves to the second. Hans came to us with convoy guards, he summoned all those who were noted and led them away. In the yard four trucks were waiting.

Hans then ordered the rest of us to prepare for a concert. It was supposed to begin exactly within an hour. Otherwise we will jump.

We decided: better to jump, but we will not sing!

Three women escaped from the construction site. How and where they went is unknown. Somebody must have helped them, because they could not have done this alone surrounded by such a large security guard and with their clothing labeled. What is amazing is that no one even noticed when they escaped. It only dawned on them when it was time to go to dinner. The guards whistled, shouted, searched, but in vain. Of course, for letting this happen the *unterscharführer* can send them to the front.

Why did I not know that they were preparing to escape? I would have asked them to take me also. I would not have been a burden to them, I would not ask them for anything, not complain, and even not eat.

Now these poor souls have their freedom. Meanwhile, no doubt, they are resting in some basement. They will wait for the Red Army. But Masha feels that they are not sitting in any basement. They did not have time to make earlier arrangements and no one helped them. It is a simple situation of an opportune moment, they took off and will attempt to travel by night in the direction of Vilnius. But the roads are increasingly being guarded and they will eventually be caught.

Is she really right?

We were not released after the evening inspection. The *unterscharführer* summoned Hans and the guilty convoy guards.

Hans returned in approximately an hour and started to capriciously inspect our alignment. We had to have an exemplary formation, because right now the chief of all the concentration camps of Latvia was to arrive.

What will occur? It is clear that not only Hans but even the *unterscharführer* was agitated.

Finally this chief arrived. Accompanied by the *unterscharführer* and his retinue he majestically marched by us, evaluating and frowningly listening to the explanations of the *unterscharführer*. Hans with little Hansik did not even attempt to get close. They also stood in line, but somewhat further and separate from us, but still in line.

The chief came up to us. He poked one girl with his lash and ordered her to step forward. He poked another, a third... He selected six in this manner. He lined them facing us. He announced that he is taking them as hostages. If those who escaped are not found within 24 hours they will be shot. Even if they are found they will nevertheless be shot. And just because this was the first occasion of such an incident in our camp, he was only going to select two for each that escaped. But if something like this should repeat the punishment will be significantly worse. We need to watch one another. If we find out that someone is making preparations to escape, tell someone. Then you will not die.

The doomed were led away.

Battles are occurring not far from Vilnius! The information is not very accurate if unconditionally based on fascist newspapers. (We often find one at the factory, in the women's toilet under the cabinet. No doubt some Latvian woman inserts it there especially for us.)

It is difficult to say where the front is right now. But one thing is clear: The Germans have withdrawn from Russia and Ukraine. Now the fighting, no doubt, is occurring somewhere in Belarus, not far from here, or even closer than we think, since the occupiers communicate their failures very late.

But here for the meanwhile there is no feeling that they are gathering to relocate. They are inhumane and cruel just as always.

We found a bottle. We shoved all my papers into it. I had to rewrite it on thinner paper and in very small letters to fit more of it.

Rewriting it I deliberately strived to write entire pieces by memory, while the girls then verified what I wrote. They praised me, saying I have a good memory. In my opinion, I just simply trained myself to do this, although in school I was compelled to do this. If I was ice skating too long and returned home late, and I had to confess to mama that I ran off to skate, and that I did not finish all my home work, I was afraid but still had to go to school not having looked in my books. If they asked me a question I had to by memory explain to the teacher what the previous lesson was and so got a passing grade. But right now I remember nothing.

We need to bury the bottle. But where? The sentry will see us. Maybe in the corner inside the wall? But we are not able to patch the hole.

More escaped! This time from the silk dress factory, and not just three, but nine persons: seven men and two girls.

There is panic in the camp. Again the same chief arrived. The *unterscharführer* is conducting himself as though insane. He is screaming at Hans, that he has no ability to straighten out "these swine." He threatens us, that we will be shot to the very last person. He scares the guards by telling them that they will be sent to the front the next day. He even scolds little Hans for the place being so dirty. After noticing the chief's car driving in, all is quiet. The *unterscharführer* runs to meet him, stretches his hand and zealously hollers, "*Heil Hitler.*" But the chief only throws some profanity at him.

We are petrified.

This time he doesn't even count, he just selects hostages. He runs through the formation and pokes people with his lash. He gets close to us. He walks toward us. He looks at me. He raises his hand. The lash falls sliding past my face and hits Masha. She takes three steps forward. They grab her! They will shoot her!

The chief walks to the men. He orders those working at the silk dress factory to form one line. He counts two, and orders the third to step forward, counts two and orders the third forward. And so to the end of the line.

Those selected make a line in front of us. Masha is also standing among them. The chief gives his address. It is our own fault. He warns us: Here everybody will answer for one person. There was no reason for anyone to escape. As long as we work, we are provided shelter and food. We only need to work and we would be able to live. But for the attempt to escape – capital punishment. Not only those who did escape as the will be caught anyway, but also us.

Black vehicles drove into the yard...

Another July 21. I am 17 years of age. My first birthday anniversary without mama and my fourth without papa. Are they no longer here? This cannot be! But maybe mama is also somewhere in a camp?

Will I survive to my next birthday? Where will I then be? It will be the end for the fascists for sure, but will I live to see it? The occupiers do not even hide this, that fighting is occurring in the area surrounding Vilnius. One Latvian woman told Liza that all the Germans have withdrawn from Vilnius, but they are not willing to admit it.

Is this really true? Does this mean there are no German soldiers on any Vilnius street? No one is being confined? They are not hauling any to Ponary? That people can go where they want without a star, and along the sidewalk? That it is quiet at Ponary? If everyone would arise from the pit and return to their home, then this would indicate that the fascists, ghetto, Murer, Kittel, *aktions* – were only one long terrifying dream.

No, not a dream. This was. No one will return from Ponary.

We were registered today. Hans assured us that they are updating the card-index, because there have been many changes in the camp recently (how cynically they label the transfer of people for execution, but they do not note this in the card file). It is not clear who remains in the camp and who does not.

Is it really this way?

My premonition did not deceive me.

During the evening inspection the *unterscharführer* started to read names off a list. Only elderly persons were listed. Those summoned were arranged, counted, and the convoy guards walked them out the gates...

They are not capable of working: they are over 50 years of age, so the excuse is that they are "being transferred to another camp."

This is the reason the card-index has to be brought up to date.

The stokers attempted to hide Suritz, an actor of the Riga theater, in the boiler fuel container, but one guard noticed them and as punishment he threatened to also haul off the stokers along with the elderly.

We were ordered to again arrange ourselves, fill the vacant spots between us and straighten the lines for inspection. I had to relocate to the next row, where just a few minutes earlier a Riga woman once stood: she was medium height, graying hair, and displayed a very intelligent posture. All that remained of her was her footprints in the sand. But I was supposed to stand exactly in the same spot, so now no more trace of her being here remained.

One more girl escaped from the silk dress factory. They said that a young Latvian boy fell in love with her and she disappeared together with him.

They do not find her. A dog was toured through the factory, but he did not smell anything. Tobacco was scattered all over.

The *unterscharführer* has gone totally insane. He beats up any person that gets close to him. Hans is already hoarse from hollering, while the guards, after hearing themselves reprimanded, unload all their malice on us: pushing and beating, and threatening to shoot us on the spot.

The chief is not coming. This means that no more hostages will be taken. All will be taken.

Although improbable, but perhaps nothing terrible will happen, only to again change our clothing and shave our hair. Of course, this is sad, but better for them to take my hair than my head. Women assure us that the Germans need working strength badly, this is why they are not shooting us.

While we stand in line at the barbers, because of these circles smeared with oil paint on our chest and back we fear pressing against each other in line so not to get paint on each other. They take their time removing the hair using electric shears. Several women are already completely bald. They look grotesque, it is difficult to recognize them. Their faces seem to be entirely different. Their heads are in some awkward and flawed form. One has a pointed head, the back of another's head is smooth.

Some of the more daring decided against allowing themselves to be disfigured. But the *unterscharführer* warned Hans that any person who avoids the new attire or shave must be put into custody, because it is obvious they are preparing to escape.

The cold electric shears slide over my head. Clumps of hair fall on my shoulders, arms and knees. If I had someplace to store them I would take a few locks as a keepsake. All of a suddenly my head is unusually cold.

I am shaved bald. Do I appear as ugly as the rest? They no doubt think the same as they look at me.

It appears they are fooling worse with the men. They are allowing them to keep some length of hair. What they are doing is shearing a band over the center of the head: from the forehead to the back of the nape. The men appear even uglier, it seems the head is divided in half. The barbers were not allowed to completely shave their hair.

Even sheep are shorn more kindly than us.

They brought Tallits into our block of barracks (white material with black stripes with which devout Jews cover themselves during prayer).[103] They were torn into pieces and distributed to us to use as scarves. In a stern manner Hans ordered us to wear these scarves not only in camp, but also at work. To bare our heads was prohibited!

This meant the fascists did not want outsiders to see how they impart their "culture" to others. They aspire to be recognized as the creators of a "new Europe," as magnanimous knights, cultural liberators, who are afraid to display their malicious activities. But I will deliberately show them! I am not at all ashamed to walk about with a bare head. Let everyone see what the fascists are up to!

I will absolutely remove my scarf! And I will also motivate others!

But my eagerness to fight led nowhere!

The convoy guards reported that as soon as we left the camp almost our entire company removed their scarves. This is just want Hans wanted. After the inspection he released the other brigades while ordered us to jump. He hit us more than

---

[103] As men wear Tallits, this is a manner of humiliation and desecration of the Jewish religion.

usual. He then chased us up the stairs to the fourth floor and down and then up, down, up, down.

I can barely move. My heard is insanely beating. My throat is dry. I have spasms in my throat, I cannot breathe, right now I will fall.

But I nonetheless do not fall. When Hans was fed up with chasing us, he again ordered us to jump. To rest we were required to march while singing and then again jump. But in order to better remember this lesson we had to run upstairs to the fourth floor and down another 10 times.

By the time he released us the entire block was fast asleep. We of course got no dinner.

I composed two announcements for the *Women's Express*. In one I stated that a new fashion just arrived from Paris and depicted in a magazine. It appears that no longer is combing or hats in fashion, only shaved heads and striped dresses. The women of Strasdenhof appear to have quickly adapted this latest fashion. In the second announcement I informed them that a new barber ship was open for business in our camp – a men's beauty salon, where the men are sheared according to the latest fashion – with wide avenues.

Many men were driven away in trucks. They say they will be chased through roads and field to clear them of mines. I asked my neighbor Ruth how this is done. She only sighed and did not reply. But Liza explained to me that the poor souls are supposed to simply walk along a field where mines are located until they step on one and fly into the air shredded into pieces.

Such a monstrous danger is beyond my ability to fathom.

Explosions woke us at night. They are bombing!

We lie, holding our breath and await new explosions. But no more. It is quiet...

In vain do we rejoice. Maybe these German themselves destroyed something or our men are being shredded stepping on mines.

When they warned us that the morning inspection will be a half-hour earlier, we did not turn any attention to it. But seeing many soldiers we got upset. What now?

Soldiers barricade all exists, they even climbed on the roofs.

The *unterscharführer's* assistant brought two boxes: one was larger, it was black; the second smaller, a bright color. He set them down and himself climbed on a stool and announced to all the regiments that those who are no longer capable of working will be transferred to another camp. These were those above 30 years of age and younger than 18.

We knew what "to be transferred" meant.

But I just turned 17 the previous week!

The *unterscharführer's* assistant takes a package of file cards from the black box and begins to call out the numbers. The male or female summoned must answer, "*Jawohl*" and walk over to the wall. The SS agent shouts the number and the doomed persons walk over to the assigned spot. Some cards he puts aside and does not announce its number, apparently people near the age limits but accepted. And again a number and again, "*Jawohl*" People move one after another, so without an end. Near me five walked out, the SS agent does not get hoarse and does not end. He talks another package. No doubt he will now summon me, he will say, "Five thousand seven." I am supposed to answer, "*Jawohl*" and walk forward... But then where?

It will be soon... Only a few cards are left in his hands. No doubt one of them is mine... It is done... No... I was about to answer, but another did ahead of me. Yes, it was not I. In fact I did not even hear the entire number, only, "Five thousand..." and I died, since my number begins with these digits.

The SS agent takes a third package. No doubt my file card lies in this one. He calls. People walk out. Soon I will go. Of my group apparently no one will remain. They should have just taken us all immediately without this torment.

The *unterscharführer's* assistant jumps from his stool! Did it finally end?

Hans ordered us into formation, we will go to work. I am trying to not catch his attention so he will not notice that I am below the lower age requirement. I feel that someone is clasping my hand, it is my neighbor-twin. We were born the same year and so both are 17. This means I am not the only one who survived. Maybe there are more of us? No, there are five of us... Accidental or a mistake?

Hans counts us three times and gives the report to the *unterscharführer*, that the total in the camp re 520 inmates. He does not include those selected, while yesterday with this same tone of voice he reported 1,300 inmates in the camp.

The brigades are now very small. I cannot imagine how we will work.

They gave us the command to go to work, while the doomed were moved to an empty building at the furthest wing.

One thought does not give me rest the entire time along the road: what is the reason for my retention? Did the *unterscharführer's* assistant skip me, or when I registered did he not hear me correctly when I said my age and so gave me a year older?[104] If I knew it would be easier for me to orient myself, what to say the next time when they decide to do this again.

The mood is miserable. Over half the workstations stand vacant. Just yesterday our women worked at them, but today...

The Latvian women look at us empathetically. They ask about their assistants, they feel sad. It even seems that the workstations are making a quieter noise...

---

[104] The Russian for 17 and 18 are similar in pronunciation.

A dead silence greeted us at the camp upon our return. Earlier all of us assembled for inspection occupied the entire floor, today we reach only to the door.

After inspection they assigned us more work. The men carried water, while we washed the floors, stairs, even the roof, washing away stains of blood.

It appears that when the doomed were routed to the vehicles the men attempted to run. They climbed over the fences, others secluded themselves in the barracks, fuel tanks, toilets. The convoy guards, shooting, ran after them. They shot them right where they were in the barracks and stairs. Two were shot and left hanging on the fence. They wanted to throw those hiding in the fuel tanks right into the fire alive with the stokers who were hiding them. The worst was dealing with a Riga man who hid in a sewer pipe. They could not remove him from there at all, so they fired high-powered bullets into him and crushed his head. Then they drug his body down the stairs and threw him into a vehicle along with the living. A lump of his brain remained in a puddle of dried blood on the stairs. We wrapped it in a sheet of paper and buried it in a hole near the wall. In place of a tombstone we placed some white rocks.

Late that night they released us back into our barrack. It was unusually empty. We spoke with our volume turned down, as though it was a wake for the deceased. We all laid down to sleep together in one corner.

Two days passed quietly.[105]

We were afraid that on Sunday they would force us to march while singing past the small grave in the corner with the white rocks on it. We barely drug through the morning inspection with our heavy hearts.

It appears that this is not what we should have feared. After inspection the *unterscharführer* announced that a

---

[105] The evacuation of Kaiserwald and Strasdenhof camps occurred August 5, 1944.

directive was received that night regarding the urgent evacuation of the camp. We well knew what "evacuation" meant in their language.

They herded us into the building where the sacrifices of the previous *aktion* occurred on Thursday. On the walls were written many familiar names. Alongside their personal data and addresses were requests for vengeance. When the people wrote this they were still alive. Now all that remains is this request.

Maybe I should leave the same type of trace of myself? Let someone at some time read it.

All of a sudden we all rushed to the doors, but no black vehicles were seem. But several transport trucks were there. Bundles of some sort were being unloaded from them. It appears this was clothing, the striped clothes of inmates, the same as what we saw at Kaiserwald.

We were told to undress entirely, only our boots and scarves remaining. Maybe indeed they will evacuate? Or maybe just an excuse in order to issue us this new attire. The women assure us that the fascists apparently are very regimented on this issue of having to so urgently evacuate. Maybe that night it was definitely ours that bombed? If they were not removing us from these premises right now we would be waiting for the Red Army. But maybe another miracle might occur, and right now as we are standing in formation the Red Army might rush in through the gates, disarm the German soldiers and we be liberated.

However... There was no Red Army, and we are standing naked in line waiting for our striped clothes. The SS agents deliberate force us to walk alongside these windows on the first floor where the glass on the windows is not painted and where the men are lined. They stand there with their eyes down. Soldiers are beating them, laughing at then and forcing them to look at us.

I received my new attire – a long and rigid shirt, the same type of pants and a striped coarse dress that is way too big for me. I am looking all over, maybe I will find a rope somewhere. I could tie it to myself so not to get entangled in this bag.

They herd us outdoors. Men are standing in our spots.

The *unterscharführer's* assistant and Hans are closing and locking all the doors. Soldiers are loading their belongings into the trucks. All are leaving. The camp is being liquidated.

The men have likewise changed clothes. These scary black trucks are driving into the yard. The SS agents are hurrying us. They hit us, push us, for us to crowd together. The trucks have no windows. It is dark, asphyxiated, but the soldiers push and shove harder, we all need to fit in them.

We stand packed, I can hardly breathe. It seems my ribs cannot handle the pressure. It is uncomfortable to just rotate my hand.

The trucks are driving out. First straight, then turning somewhere, then rushing further and further. I am exhausted. My feet do not hold me up, I am falling. If they would just for a minute stop and open the doors!

Finally we arrive. We are at some ocean port. They again arrange us, count us again and herd us into a large ship. It is apparently a military vessel, because from under the canopies the barrels of guns are sticking out. Cargo is being loaded onto the ship. The women assume that the Germans are loading the equipment from their workstations and other expensive items.

They chase us onto the ship. The deck is as large as a city square. The convoy guards open the hatches and order us to climb down. The narrow ladder is very steep, it is dark below. I descend. More narrow ladders and the guard is herding us lower.

Finally we are at the very bottom. By touch I find a place to sit. Somehow I find a spot and sit. It appears many women are here. They are from other camps.

Where are they taking us? Will it be worst than what we already endured? What is primary is that we are distancing ourselves from the front.

We sit. Maybe on the outside of the ship time is moving along, but here it seems to have stopped. Is it still day or already night?

My lips are emaciated, I so much want a sip of water. It is hot, stuffy, my shirt irritates my neck and underarms causing pain, but I am afraid to remove it. I could lose it in the dark. At least to stretch my legs...

We are still not in despair. Why is it taking them so long to load? What is it that they are moving from here?

Those sitting closer to the exit started to bang on the lid of the hatch, asking for water. For a long while no one answers, then the hatch opens and a guard maliciously shouts, "Whoever is hollering will be thrown overboard! You can have all the water you want!"

The hatch slammed shut. It is dark again.

Finally the ship departs. We are sailing. Where? Will we ever return?

Some of the girls who returned from the deck informed us that it was morning. It appears a somewhat talkative sentry was standing on guard and he decided to remove those who fainted.

I would have wanted to also go on deck, but those in worse of a condition than mine were allowed ahead of me. There were also some who deliberately feigned losing consciousness.

A girl next to me proposed creating a three-some. She will "faint" and two of us will carry her out. I said I was not good at pretending, better for me to carry another.

Finally, fresh air! I breathe it deeply-deeply. The sun is blinding my eyes, the wind is refreshing me! So wide the expanse: only sun, sea and sky. In the distance something can be seen. No doubt a city. Maybe Klaipeda?[106] I was born there.

"Return!" hollered a German. So soon. Our sick girl opened her eyes much too soon.

They did not allow us on deck at night. We sat withered, sweaty.

Unexpectedly from above we heard a German soldier's voice. "Air raid alarm! Do not move or we will shoot!" How can we move? And who will notice us from an airplane? What a joke.

Soon the alarm ended. It is obvious that the airplanes just flew by.

In the morning they brought some bread. They were too lazy to distribute it and just threw it down to us. Some got a few pieces, while others like myself got nothing. The more fortunate ones shared with us. Someone shoved a small piece into my hand, I grabbed it so at least I got four morsels.

The intolerably long day ended, passed and now the difficult night.

About noon the next day we sensed the ship was slowing its speed. It stopped. But they were not releasing us. Are we to travel further? Then for sure we will all suffocate.

Finally we heard the words of salvation, "*Heraus!*"[107]

When we landed on shore I looked around: it was nothing like a port. Just some fields and roads and some small homes.

Some teenagers ran to look at us. One of us in a whisper asked where we were. They answered, that Danzig[108] was not far from here. But somehow where we were did not interest me, what was important was for me to breath.

They counted us again and ordered us to walk. We reached some river. It was getting dark. They started to herd us into

---

[106] A city in Lithuania on the Baltic Sea coast.
[107] "Get out!"
[108] Today known as Gdansk, Poland, on the Baltic Sea coast.

some covered black barges. Again the sea.[109] The first group crawled in bent over and somehow sat while the convoy guards shoved more in. They scared us by saying that anybody who would not fit would be thrown in the water. Cramped and exhausted, we sailed.

The entire night was a nightmare for me. Several occasions I felt I was already dying, some moments I was unconscious.

The sun was already high when they chased us out and onto the shore. We were hardly able to catch our breath as they herded us further.

At one intersection there was a sign with the inscription: Stutthof.[110] This meant we were being taken there.

We walk through a clean village. On each side of the street small houses slumber in the sun's light. Each is surrounded by a little fence filled with flowers. Children are playing... It is so quiet here! As if there is no war, no Hitler, no Ponary anywhere in the world.

Long rows of barracks can be seen in the distance. We turned to the right and a beautiful garden blocked the view of the barracks. Beautiful avenues, little stone houses, fountains, swings, a table for ping-pong, a genuine corner of paradise. But the garden ended and a desolate field was unveiled in front of us, barricaded by a barbwire fence and long rows of barracks. They were as if built on sand, separated from one another by rows of wire fencing. It seems the camp is divided into immense transparent wire cages. On high towers looking down on the fences were the booths of the sentries with windows facing all four directions.

Officers stand at the gates. They count us and allow us inside. At the entrance a sentry warns us in a monotone voice that it is forbidden to get near a fence, it is electrified.

---

[109] Probably the Vistula Lagoon.
[110] Concentration camp near the city of Sztutowo, outside of Gdansk.

We enter the first cage. The gate closes behind us. The next opens into the same type of cage. It also closes. They release us into the third cage. And so we go further, deeper into the camp.

As we walk alongside the barracks the inmates start to talk to us, asking us where we are from. Although the security guards beat us for talking we do not restrain ourselves and reply. They speak to us from the barracks in Russian, Polish and Hebrew. These horribly emaciated women, obviously sick, stand at one barrack. They do not ask us about anything, they only advise us to watch out for a certain Marx.

To the right from the women's, are the men's barracks. The fence between them is double: two rows of barbwire. They are separated by a wide space. Other than this, on the inside of the barriers beginning at the towers the tops have an additional row of stretched barbwire that is inclined inward.

The men are also asking about us. Occasionally someone will dare to squeak, asking our origin. In one spot some aged man, hearing that we are from Vilnius, asks how long we have been absent from there. His face seems to me to be very familiar, but to gaze at him closer is dangerous, the guard is right next to me.

They lead us to the very last barracks: numbers 19 and 20. Several SS agents, and one civilian with the number of an inmate on him, are already standing there. No sooner does this civilian shout at us to arrange ourselves in formation for inspection that he starts to beat and kick us. Why? We are getting in line, and he did not order us to do anything else.

I stretched and then stood still. But this civilian villain flew at me and I did not have enough time to figure at whom he was aiming that I doubled up from this horrible pain. While the SS agents stood to the side and laughed.

This monster beat us all up, from one end of the line to the other, then he combed his hair, tucked his shirt back in, and started to count. But now one officer noticed that it was time for lunch and they left, leaving us standing.

At the other end of the formation several dozen women stand. They are explaining their life here, and each of them just whispers to the next and who passes on the message. They are from Poland. They were only in these blocks a week, they were in others earlier. It is worse here because the supervisor of these blocks is Marx, the very one who just beat up all of us. He is the devil in the disguise of a human. He has already beat several to death. He is an inmate himself, sitting here a year so far for the murder of his wife and children. The SS agents love him because of his unheard of cruelty.

So this is the meaning of a genuine concentration camp! My conclusion is that Strasdenhof was still relatively tolerable.

The SS agents and Marx returned toward evening. Beating and cursing he somehow counted us and released us into the barrack. The bunk beds here are also three high, but without straw mattresses and blankets. They are plain wood planks.

Marx's cry arouses us. Rocks are flying through an opened window. We rush to the door. Crowding, pushing. Unexpectedly all of us back away: Marx stands at the door and hits each person on the head as she exits. We want to jump through the window, but Marx obviously guessed our intentions and is already running there, to beat us for "violation of order." Don't we know that we need to exit through the door?

I run back to the door and barely evade Marx's hit, although he got back here by this time.

As punishment for not running to inspection fast enough, Marx leaves us to stand in the heat the entire day. He warns us, that in the event of the smallest motion the sentries will shoot.

The sun is pitilessly baking us and not at all moving from its place, it just gets higher and higher. I want to drink. My feet shake and ready to collapse. I want to fall right here in the sand, in the dirt, just to get a minute's rest.

They registered us. I am afraid to record my actual age, as they consider those who are under 18 years of age to be incapable of working. I thought about listing my age as 20, but what if the SS agent does not believe me? For the attempt of a deception they will surely shoot me. But fortunately he did not even raise his head to look at me.

They gave us numbers imprinted on small pieces of cloth and ordered us to quickly sew them to our clothing. They especially brought us needles and thread for this.

I am no longer Number 5007; I am now Number 60821.

After registration they served us soup. Here it is worse than at Strasdenhof. It is plain warm dirty water without even one kernel of anything. Some girls got it good as they found a piece of a potato peel in theirs.

We have been in this camp nine days. In every aspect it is worse than Strasdenhof. Marx bestially beats people, all of us walk about black and blue. There are no un-marked bodies. I call these bruises – Marx's autographs. Some women are angry that I can still make a joke out of something. I do not do this intentionally, it just occurs on its own.

The entire day, from morning inspection to the evening, to enter the barrack is prohibited. If Marx does not order us to stand "contritely" or on our knees, we sit on the ground, in the dust, in direct sunlight. There is no shade here in which to hide. They do not give us anything to drink, if you do not count the morning "coffee" – a small bowl divided among five.

The SS agents already selected sacrifices for the crematorium from our block. They arrange us, inspect us, and the worst appearing they lead away. On each of the initial two occasions they took 30 persons, while a few days ago it was 60. No one seems to know where the crematorium is. They say it is somewhere near the entrance.

One gossiper over soup related to us Vilnius residents that Balys Sruoga gives us his regards.[111] So this is the face that seemed so familiar to me! It is not a surprise that I did not immediately recognize him. I only saw his photographs in textbooks, and there he, of course, was not attired in an inmate's uniform and was not so emaciated.

It seems to me that I saw A.R. and my father on the men's side. But now the more I look I no longer see them. It is far anyway and difficult to ascertain. But maybe this was not him? I plainly want to feel he is alive, so do I imagine this.

SS agents arrived dressed in black attire. They ordered us to get arranged and one by one to walk past them showing our legs. They would set to the side any person who had many abscesses on his legs. But if someone has relatively few abscesses the person was further inspected, the arms and hands.

I fell into the category of the stronger. We were arranged and counted. Two at the very end were moved over to the other group so that an even number of 300 would remain.

The security guard opened the gate that led us into a neighboring department. We sighed with relief: at least we will be further from the horrible Marx.

Now we are also separated from the others by a wire fence. They, the unfortunates, stand at the barricade and stare enviously at us: we will go to work while they will remain here.

Someone released a rumor that they will send us into the forest, to the peasants. The officers discussed this among themselves. But it cannot get worse.

The rumor it seems was confirmed.

The security guard arrived. He took ten women and asked if they were able to milk cows. All, of course, quickly confirmed that they were able.

---

111 Balys Sruoga, 1896-1947, Lithuanian playwright and poet. He survived and wrote a popular book on his experiences at the camp.

But what if they ask me? If I tell them the truth, they will no take me. I will lie that I can, and if they discover I cannot, then back to the camp. What should I do? I ask others what they will say. But the women just laugh at my doubts.

The security guard led out 36 women, myself among them. They distributed to each of us a torn military blanket. Some kind of people were waiting at the gate. They started to pick whom them wanted.

They inspect us, feel our arms, ask if we are lazy. Two girls are weeping, they are sisters and do not want to be separated. One boss selected one and another boss selected the other. They ask if they can be sent together because of their entire family only the two remain.

No one is paying attention to me, all just walk by. I guess they will not select me and I will return to this hell. Maybe I should ask to be taken? Others are doing this. I say, "*Ich bin stark,*" – "I am strong." But no one hears me. "*Ich bin stark,*" I repeat even louder. "What, what?" says some older gentleman. I begin to quickly tell him that I want to work, that I am not lazy. "*Ja, gut!*" he says and walks away. But apparently he reflects on the matter and returns. He takes me to the side where three other selected women are already standing.

The convoy guard approaches, records our numbers and orders us to follow the boss.

We follow the same road that led us here. The little houses are comfortably resting under the sun's rays. We sit in a narrow-gauge railroad car. The convoy guard does not take his eyes off of us. The reflection of the light on his bayonet shines formidably right on my face.

Our boss is a short, bow-legged and bald, elderly man. His eyes are barely narrow slits, while his voice is hoarse and mean. It is obvious he is not satisfied with us. He is complaining to the convoy guard that he will get no benefit from workers like us. He already had four just like us, they were from Hungary, but soon became weak, and so they had to take them straight to the crematorium.

So where have I ended up! Stupid me, and I even asked to do this.

The train stopped and we got out. It appears the boss left his two-wheeled cart at the train station. The guard tied our hands together and also tied us to each other. He sat alongside the boss and we departed.

The rested horse trotted along. We were supposed to run behind them otherwise the ropes would cut into our bodies. We got tired, we could hardly breathe, but were afraid to show this. The boss will say that we are weak and will immediately send us back and then to the crematorium. These seven kilometers seem so long.[112]

Finally we turned onto a narrow trail, drove past ponds and arrived at this large yard. The house was majestic, the garden was turning green, a shed, barn and stable stood in the distance. It was obvious he was a successful businessman.

The boss once more verified our numbers and signed for receiving us from the guard. Untying our hands, he read to us the rules: we are responsible to work well and conscientiously, not to do any sabotage and not to attempt to escape. For sabotage he will send us directly to the crematorium, and with the attempt to escape he will shoot us on the spot. Scaring us this way he led us to our assigned cell. It was located in this shed at the very end, half-dark as the light only penetrated through a tiny window where a lot of flies were sitting. On the other side of the wall pigs were grunting. We had no straw mattresses or pillows, only some straw thrown into the corner. "This will be your bedroom." To ask for a mattress would be foolish, he would not provide one anyway. I dared to tell him that we were very hungry, that we did not yet eat that day. The boss turned around and ordered us to follow him. In the patio he ordered us to remove our boots, we can only enter the

---

[112] About 5 miles.

kitchen barefooted. We are categorically forbidden to enter any of the rooms. I need to tell this to my friends.

He asked the housekeeper if anything remained from lunch, then the boss started to reprimand her telling her that she cooks way too much. He then asked her to find out from his sisters if there were enough potatoes to give away. One mistress came, and she was the same kind of narrow-minded and gloomy person as the boss. She moaned saying that we were going to eat them out of house and home, but nevertheless, she stuck her nose into this kettle and decided to give us what was left.

Each of us got three whole potatoes.

"*Aufstegen!*"[113] hollered our boss. Why? It is too early. We just went to bed. Early in the morning our new boss unlocked the door and released us to wash. He stood behind us so we would not escape.

The sun was just starting to rise. It was cold. But he is in a hurry, it was almost 4 o'clock. We are supposed to start work at half-past four: carry wood, water, rake the yard, clean the furrows in the garden. Breakfast is at half-past five, and at six we are on our way to the field.

After explaining what had to be done, he gave us our food for the week: one loaf of bread with a quarter of a stick of margarine. The boss warned us that this needs to last until the following Friday. We will not get any more bread, this is our allotment. We will get coffee in the kitchen each morning, and a bowl of soup for lunch. If they can they will give us leftover potatoes for dinner, but not every evening. Only one of us at a time has the right to enter the kitchen, and she will get enough for all four of us.

We decided to each eat one slice of bread a day and then only at breakfast. But how can we restrain ourselves when this is the first occasion over such a long time that we got an entire

---

[113] "Get up!"

loaf! Maybe we should eat more today to regather our strength and then decrease later? So we took a piece, and then another, and a good thing the boss came to summon us to the field or else we would have eaten the entire loaf.

The boss rides horseback while we drag along behind him. It appears we are not the only persons here. There is this Ukrainian Ivan with his wife and three children (the occupiers removed them before the retreat), a French prisoner-of-war, and a Polish woman Zosya, a I girl Raya who believed in Hitler's promised paradise in Germany and voluntarily enlisted for work, now she is killing herself, weeping, but of course they will not let her return.[114]

The fields on each side of the road belong to our boss. He is probably an SS agent or plainly some kind of activist, because often at night he will take his machine gun and go riding on his bicycle to certain kinds of meetings or just nighttime excursions. He is very mean and a frugal old bachelor, while his sisters – old maids – are plain witches. They go insane if they have to give a plate of soup to Ivan's children, who do not work. But still they occasionally give the older one, who is a seven-year old boy, work, but is it always beyond his infantile strength.

All of this we ascertained from Ivan as we waked to the field.

As soon as we arrived the boss immediately put us to work. The Frenchman mows the rye while we follow behind and tie in it sheaves.

At first it seemed this was not difficult, but it did prick our hands, but soon our pricked hands started to hurt. Our waists also started to hurt.

When can we rest? It appears only at noon, during lunch. How much longer do I have to wait? Ivan defines time by

---

[114] There is a play on words here as the Russian name Raya is also the word for paradise.

looking at a shadow. Right now it is only 10 o'clock. Then a long stretch until evening! Maybe I can have a conversation with the Frenchman? He of course will enjoy it. But what can I tell him if all the French words that I learned in school have vaporized from my memory? Maybe I can ask him what time it is. This I remember.

I gather and gather until finally lunch arrived. They brought soup to us so we would not waste time in transit to the kitchen and back. The Frenchman, not suspecting my intentions, left with his bowl to a shady place.

We did not even finish eating by the time the boss is already urging us to return to work. He could not give us enough time to rest!

So how do I start a conversation with the Frenchman? A few times I started to sing *Frere Jacques*,[115] but I could not remember anything else and he did not turn his attention to me. Either he did not hear or pretended he did not hear.

Soon the pain masked all my thoughts. My pricked hands are swollen, reddened, it is horrible to look at them. While my waist looks like it was pierced by a bayonet. I want to drink so much. The hunger is eating away at the pit of my stomach, although I did eat today, and had some bread and almost real potato soup. Ivan taught me how to shell the ears, but to do this occasionally, otherwise we will fall behind the mower. Ivan is complaining: If the Frenchman only knew Russian we would ask him not to hurry. But when we try to use sign language he cannot decipher it. I offered my services as a translator.

The Frenchman was overjoyed at hearing his native language and started to quickly explain something to me. I was barely able to decipher a few words, I asked him to speak slower, because my French is very weak. I related to him our common request to not work at such a tempo.

It became easier: the Frenchman whistled while he worked, and if he noticed we were getting behind he would wait. We

---

[115] A French nursery rhyme.

feared for our Raya, that the boss will notice and accuse us of sabotage. But the Frenchman is not stupid: if he sees the boss approaching he immediately picks up the pace.

The sun already descended to the horizon, but the boss mentioned nothing about releasing us. Not a surprise to us, as our predecessors knuckled under, we likewise will knuckle under.

At the final end the boss announced that it was half-past eight, and we can end our work. We slowly drug ourselves to our shed.

Sunday was a day of rest for everyone except us. We needed to haul not only wood and water, rake the yard, clean the furrows in the garden, but also give feed to the cattle and carefully clean the holiday carriage, in which the boss would solemnly drive to church.

After lunch the Frenchman went to his friend who worked not too far from here, Ivan's wife would wash their clothes, while Zosya would just sleep: she did not sleep the entire night again, weeping. The boss locked us and, placing his machine gun behind his shoulder, drove off somewhere.

It is a quiet Sunday afternoon. Even the leaves of the trees lazily slumber in the sun. Birds were not flying. All were resting.

Borrowing from Ivan's wife a pair of scissors, a needle and thread we embellished ourselves: we shortened and mended our clothes. Tanya knows how to sew and this helps us. From cut strips of cloth we all sewed brassieres for ourselves. I do not need one as I am so skinny.

If it were not for the crimson-faced[116] Raya we could forget about things for one minute, not to agonize our heart. But she cannot be silent, not for one minute. This is already the third time in the same number of days that she explains to us, and with new details, how she lost her child.

---

[116] The adjective of the city Riga is also the same word as crimson in Russian.

At the Riga ghetto she was still with her husband and child. When they heard they were taking the children, they decided to end it all. The husband gave injections to the child, then her and then himself.

Sadly the two of them recovered, but the child was gone. They did not even hear when he was taken. Now the incident tortures her, the fear that her child perhaps awoke before they did and cried in fear trying to wake them, but they did not hear anything. Maybe the executioners beat him, or played with him in their hands, or maybe he escaped from them.

The husband almost lost his mind. He could not at all understand why the poison did not work.

So how do you comfort her? We tell her that doses sufficient for an adult would definitely be enough to kill a child. We comfort her by convincing her that her child died!

That evening the boss took us to milk cows. This is what I feared the entire time! I just hoped the cow would be calm.

The other two mistresses came along to watch so we do not drink any of the milk.

I stretch, stretch, but not a drop of milk. The cow is getting mean, right now it will kick me. I pull on it harder. A few drops trickled, but they flowed down my hand to my elbow. Suddenly I felt someone kick me. The mistress treated me to a kick in the side, and I flew into the cow's stomach. I needed to get moving.

I watched the others, they are succeeding, especially Tanya. The genuinely golden hands of this girl led me to conclude that all she did her entire life was to milk cows and nothing else. I watched how she held her fingers and pulled. The milk in two joyful streams hit the bottom of the pail.

We milked all the cows – 27 of them. At the end my hands were shaking so much that I could not get them to do what I wanted anymore.

I did not sleep that night: I put my hands this way and that way and they still hurt.

We are bringing in the rye. This is how it is for me. When we
loaded the first wagon the boss ordered me to ride the horse,
there are four of them to pull the wagon, and drive them home.
But how can I get into the saddle when my height reaches only
half-way up the horses' stomach and never in my life have I
even ridden a horse? The Frenchman apparently noticed this
about me and since I was still young, so he helped me up and
started to quickly explain. If he did not talk so fast, for sure I
would have understood twice of what I heard. Finally I realized
that he was talking about the house, wood fence and horses. He
teaches me how to get off the horse, advises me to get as far as
the wood fence, move to the fence and then jump down. *"Merci,"*
I tell him.

We are gathering flax. I never imagined that it was so
tasty! Tanya orders me to chew it longer; it contains oil which
our bodies have long not had. If we were to settle for what they
gave us we would have given in long ago, especially under such
heavy work.

The boss is constantly hurrying us, driving us, not giving us
a minute to rest. Zosya figured how to deal with him. It
appears the boss has this fear of a woman's nakedness, and
when he comes to wake us Zosya gives him the impression she
is throwing the blanket off of herself. The old man shoots out
like a bullet and she gets a little more rest.

Now when the boss' urging becomes intolerable we take
advantage of it. We give him the impression it is very hot,
remove our dresses and work wearing solely our shirts. The
boss curses us, runs back and forth, stands with his back to us,
hollers at us to dress. But we pretend that we do not hear, or
respond in an innocent manner that it is very hot and we will
work faster if wearing less. The old man sits spitefully in a
canal along the road and leaves.

Battles against the German armies are occurring not far away. The boss' neighbors were talking about it. Among other things they are very humane. Maybe because they are poor. They do not own land of their own but make a living working on the estates of their rich neighbors. But their manner of income is rather strange. For their help during harvest our boss allows them to glean, to gather at the picked field or from the truck what falls. They wander all day long, bent over in the stubble, gathering ears of grain into sacks.

When the boss is not nearby they talk with us, they tell us of the news at the front. Once they even shared with us their family tragedies: one son is a communist and languishes in some concentration camp (and maybe he is not even alive anymore), while the second son is an SS agent, a watchman at the same camp. Of course in public he denies his brother. He does not visit the parents, he is ashamed that they are so poor and that the father's vocation was making wooden shoes.

News of the approaching front has stirred up slumbering hopes. If only the Red Army would get here the sooner!

It is already cold. Especially in the morning. Nothing surprising, it is October. Autumn. We shiver, our teeth chatter, but the boss does not notice this. We asked him for some linsey-woolsey cloths, but he barked at us, saying that the clothes we received at the camp should be sufficient.

We bundle ourselves in our blankets. It is still cold, the blanket gets wet from the rain, and our feet freeze, even though we cover them with beet stems. At night we sleep under soaking wet blankets. We asked the boss to give us more straw to bury ourselves in it, but the malicious old man would not. And through the cracks this cold wind blows. We lay there shivering, shaking, and so difficult to fall asleep.

How good the boss' dogs have it! They sleep in warmth and eat to their full. Yes, they have "a dog's life."

Now what? Work is coming to its end. The potatoes are dug up; the beets are harvested. Now we are plucking feathers, then we will wash the linen and then chop cabbage. What is next? We will not be needed, and the unneeded are discarded into the crematorium.

So regardless, I guess that we will still not escape our fate?

We wash linen. This is the second day we stand at this large tub and infinitely scrub many bed sheets, pillowcases and blankets. I have scrubbed the skin off my fingers. The boss does not give us a washboard, he seems to have no pity on our hands!

The first snow of the season fell. My feet are blue from the cold. Ivan's wife lent us a pair of stockings (and she only has two pair). We will take turns wearing them, alternating every day, beginning with the oldest. I will get to wear them day after tomorrow.

They are returning us to the camp.

Zosya heard the boss explaining that a directive was issued to return them by November 15.

Two days remains. This means that our hopes that went up are now going down.

The final morning.

How quickly did these three months speed by! Obviously because we lived almost calmly and death did not seem so inevitable. But now we are again drawing closer to it.

Ivan said that two girls who worked at a neighbor's farm hanged themselves, so not to return to the camp.

They give each of us two slices of bread for the road. The boss takes his machine gun and leads us. Ivan's wife is sobbing, the Frenchman waves with his cane a long while.

We walk alongside the pond. The water in it now seems to be dirty. The trees bid farewell to us by throwing their final leaves under our feet. They sadly rustle.

All will remain here. The trees, the road, the pond. They will be here next year and in 10 years. Nature exists infinitely relative to a human. And especially – us.

Many of our camp are at the station. The bosses hand all of them to the convoy guards. Our boss also receives a receipt, that four inmates were received from him. He tells the guard, "*Heil Hitler!*" and walks away, not even bothering to look back.

They also brought the two who hanged themselves.

It is already dark by the time we get to the camp. Again the gates open and close. We are back in the cage.

The are counting torturously long: the numbers do not add. Every row is checked, they beat each person if it appears he is not standing evenly. Again we are counted and again they cruelly curse us. Apparently they forgot about the deceased. But who will remind them of this?

It is totally dark. The watchmen are insane. Finally someone was bold enough to say, "*Zwei sind tot!*" ("Two are dead.")

The officer was agitated at such imprudence and demanded the one who shouted to be produced. He rushed out of formation, he got 10 lashes. But the reminder nonetheless helped: they quickly released us to the barrack.

In the weak light of a bulb we saw an eerie picture: on one half of the barrack, right on the floor, in four rows, these unclothed women were sleeping, tightly packed against each other. The head of one at the feet of another. Horribly stuffy, stinking. Someone hollered, "Turn around." And all of us, pushing each other, turned. Now they are laying with their faces toward us. Some woke, they stare at us. We are standing, devastated and scared.

The watchwoman flew at us and started to whip us. This meant we had to lie down and pack ourselves in the same manner for all to fit.

I cannot fall asleep. And it seems no one is sleeping on this side of the entrance. We softly speak with them. Have they been here long? Eleven months. Are they sent to work? A few groups were sent to dig ditches, but they worked there up to their waist in water, their feet would freeze, and after work they were driven straight to the crematorium. And then other new persons were sent in their place.

It is really true? Or maybe they are exaggerating? No doubt our boss had other girls working for him who could not endure. But we were more hardy.

Lice descended on us. We started to reprimand those women for releasing these insects and having them migrate on us. It appears they are not to blame; there is no water here.

I need to get out! I need to absolutely get out of here! Even to dig ditches, break rocks, anything not to remain here!

An SS agent in a black uniform came to us the next day. He started to select the stronger among us. Figuring that he was assembling a group for work all rushed toward him with a shout that they are healthy and want to work. Initially the SS agent was confused, but he got his scruples together and started to push them to the left and right getting them away from him. But he could not get order, the hunger to get out of there overcame their fears. Only when he pulled out his revolver did he succeed in forcing us back.

Selecting 500 women he led them out. I remained.

With the subsequent assembly I was able to get selected and felt myself almost happy. One way or another I will escape!

They took us to the bathhouse, ordered us to undress, and we entered this large waiting room. We petrified when we entered: these horribly emaciated and feeble women were sitting and even lying right on the concrete floor, they were almost skeletons with frantic eyes due to fear. Seeing the watchwoman behind our backs, the women started to babble out of fear, saying that they are healthy, can work and asked to be spared. They stretched their hands toward us so we would help them stand, then the watchwoman would be assured that they can still work.

I stepped forward to help a woman sitting near me, but the watchwoman shoved me back.

Authoritatively dictating she orders us not to start a panic. All will be washed and returned to the camp. When we recover our strength we will return to work. All must bathe without exception: no one dirty will be allowed back into camp.

She orders us to undress these women and carry them into to adjoining room, under the showers.

The nauseating stench affects me bad. I want to remove the dress from this one woman but she cannot stand: her feet will not hold her. I attempt to pick her up, but she moans so bad from the pain that I withdraw. What am I to do? I look at the others. It appears they are fumbling about worse than I. The watchwoman gives us scissors: if we cannot remove the clothing we need to cut it off of them.

The scissors pass from hand to hand. Now my turn. I cut the dress. Under it she is so frail that I am afraid to touch her. She is solely bones covered by dry wrinkled skin.

The woman will not allow me to remove her boots, it will be too painful. I promise to cut them from the top, but she does not allow me to touch them. Two weeks she has not removed her boots because her frostbitten and suppurated feet are stuck to the fabric.

What am I to do? Others have removed some, I still cannot finish with just her. The watchwoman obviously noticed this. She runs to me, hits me on the head and grabs the unfortunate woman by the feet. An agonizing heart-wrenching cry. I look, in the watchwoman's hand are the boots with pieces of decaying meat stuck to the fabric. I got nauseous. The watchwoman shouts at me, that I did not properly understand her. She says I have weak nerves, that I am no better in any way than any of these ill women.

I move over to undress the next woman.

We lead those who can walk, those lying we carry and place under the shower. Washing them a little we carry them back into the cold waiting room, and again place them on the cold concrete floor. No towels. The unfortunate women's teeth chatter. We are also shivering, we have to run wet from the waiting room into the shower and back [until all were bathed].

When the watchwoman turned away I asked one woman of her origin. From Czechoslovakia. A doctor. They brought her to Stutthof to work, the same reason as us. They dug ditches. They worked standing in water up to their waist. They slept on the ground. When their frostbitten hands and feet started to form abscesses they were returned to the camp. Others were taken to dig ditches. The same fate awaits them.

So this is where the group of women were taken a few days ago! And we envied them.

After we all bathed they herded us out of there, gave us disinfected dresses and led us back into the barrack. Leaving we heard the cry of the unfortunates. It was apparent they were being dragged out of there, and of course not into the camp.

So why did we have to undress them, wash them?

I could not close my eyes the entire night. This horrifying image was in front of me the entire time.

Time stretches very slowly.

It is piercingly cold. The torture standing for inspection in the mornings and evenings! Snowdrifts pile on us, a cold wind blows penetrating right through us. But we need to stand solely in our dresses and wait until the SS agents get around to arriving and counting us. Some women collapse each morning and evening.

A few days ago one woman could no longer endure and she threw herself on the electric fence. This was the sole manner of suicide, but this only shook her up. The girls supposed that the sentry noticed it soon enough and cut off the current. Finding out about this the watchwoman beat up the unfortunate woman. She shouted at her that no one has the right to act this way, "Life belongs to the Lord God!"[117] But yet this same watchwoman conceived of a Sunday amusement. It was autumn and we were working in the village and returned to camp. After lunch and together with other watchwomen she chose this one weak and frail woman and pushed her against the fence. They took bets between themselves as to how many times she would survive the shock from being pushed against the fence until she collapsed dead on the wire. (Initially the shock would just agitate and repel them.)

The place is horribly filthy. They do not give us water. The wash basins are off. A terrible thirst prevails. What they call soup is where occasionally a decayed piece of a cabbage leaf or a peel from a rotten sweet potato falls into the bowl. The taste is piercing as though pepper was dumped into it. It stings and dries the mouth. We suck on dirty trampled snow. In the barrack there is a deep hole dug that is used instead of a toilet. They do not give us a board with which to cover it. The edges are slippery. Recently one woman fell into the hole. We drug her out of there.

Nothing is heard about the advance of the Red Army.

Several officers arrived. They started to inspect us. We became happy: of course they will put us to work!

Horrible confusion ensued, each attempted to be selected. But the SS agents are dissatisfied, frowning, "They are all ready for the grave anyway." They took a few although not being very selective.

I was one of those selected. Maybe this time they will not have me undress others and will indeed send me to work.

We were supplemented to a larger group brought from other barracks. They counted a thousand in all and led us to the bathhouse, the same room where we recently undressed the

---

[117] Interesting paradox for a guard at an extermination camp to say this.

unfortunate women. Maybe they will soon lead us here in the same condition?

I froze under the cold shower, there we received clean shirts, striped dresses and the same kind of striped jackets. Our identification numbers were inscribed on them and they led us to some incompletely-built barrack. There were no doors and the windows were not yet installed, the wind blew bringing snow into it.

When it became dark they brought torn soldiers' blankets and shawls. They announced that we would spend the night here, in this barrack. We will go to work only tomorrow.

No floor, the ground was frozen, bits of wood lay all over, nails, but we still need to lie down: standing is prohibited.

The night was very long. The cold locked all of our joints, there was no hope of falling asleep. If morning would come the sooner! I attempt to imagine what the new camp will look like, what we will do there. Will we dig trenches? We need to somehow save the strength of our legs. Maybe I will find there an old sheet of paper and keep it? I will absolutely remove my boots each day. Maybe the soup there will be better? It is possible, and they will provide water, and we will wash after. Of course it cannot be worse than here.

How was I able to endure almost a month here so far? When we registered I noticed that the date inscribed on the page was November 11.

We heard the normal command, "*Aufstehen!*" – "Time to rise!"

The same watchman verified us against his list and, convinced we were all here, led us out. But strange, not to the gates, but back, to the [bathhouse] where we got our clothes. He ordered us to return our blankets, jackets and dresses. Who was slow or dared ask why received a hit on the head.

They then returned us to that same stinking barrack which we left yesterday with our original clothes.

It appears they did not take us to work because an epidemic of typhus started in the camp. We are quarantined. The camp is closed.

Epidemic! This will consume us all, regardless of age or appearance. Typhus is not selective. Of course, there is no one here to care for us. Maybe they deliberately infected the camp so we would all die. Didn't we get sick from that horrible soup? Maybe the bitter taste was not from pepper after all?

How can I protect myself? How can I get the strength to not eat this soup, our sole nourishment? How can I train myself to eat nothing at all, even not to suck on this dirty snow? But will this help any?

I feel I am getting ill. My head is heavy and howls. During inspection they support me, holding me by the arms so I do not fall. Could this be typhus? I was in pain.

The women explained to me that while I was delirious I was singing these tunes and also horribly cursing the Germans. They never suspected that I knew such abusive words. It is good my voice is weak, and that no German soldiers entered, fearing they would be infected. If they heard these words coming out of me they would have shot me on the spot.

It is uncomfortable for me that I was cursing. I explain that at home in our family this never occurred. Papa was an attorney. The women just smiled at my explanation.

They said I was hallucinating. I was seriously ill. But it seems to me they are mistaken. This apparently was something else, and not typhus, since typhus is a horrible illness! Since those who die from this are often stronger than I. If it was, then I would not have recovered so easily, without medicine. But the women explained that typhus likewise defeats the strong, those who have never been ill, since their bodies have never developed any immunity.

My mother would know, as she survived scarlet fever, yellow fever, and pleurisy when I was a child.

To wash myself with snow I crawled outside on all fours. I cannot stand as I have these green circles blurring my eyes.

This place is become a genuine extermination camp. The German soldiers no longer care about protocol. There is no more inspection: they are afraid to go outside. No food. Even what they call soup is provided only once every two or three days. Sometimes in lieu of it they bring each of us two frostbitten potatoes. We have not seen bread in a long while. I want to eat so bad, I feel myself recovering.

The lice are exasperating. We can only press them, but sadly there are no less of them.

The beauty Ruth died. Her legs started to abscess, then her arms, and so she died. She could not rise the concluding stage of her life. But even when we were at Strasdenhof she was such a beauty. Always vigilant, never displaying a bad disposition. She believed so much that we will greet the liberation and that she would be with her husband. Now she is horribly swollen and they will shove her into the crematorium oven. The end. Young, pretty, loving life, and now transformed into ashes.

Someone confirmed that it is already the new year. I heard how one sentry gave a New Year's congratulation to a watchman.

This means it is already 1945. Surely the war will end this year. The German army is being defeated. But... Not in vain do people say that a fatally wounded animal is twice as dangerous. Will we be its posthumous sacrifices? This cannot be! Why should I think that they have to kill us as they retreat? And what if they don't succeed? Then we will be free! Maybe mama and the children are at some camp? They will also be liberated. And papa will return. And Miriam will await us in Vilnius. We will all meet at our old apartment. I will again hurry to school every morning, and Miriam to the university. Rayechka and Ruvik will submerse themselves in school, now they are teenagers. But when will this occur? And will this pertain to everybody?

Raya, with whom we worked together at the farmer's, related that she heard from the distributor of our soup that there was a fire at the crematorium. The shed containing the fuel burned down. They assume it was arson.

This will nonetheless not save us.

Exasperation! I slept pressed into a corpse. At night of course I did not sense this. It was very cold and I pressed myself into my bed partner's back. I placed her hands under my arms. It seems she moved, grabbing them. But in the morning it was apparent she had died during the night.

The watchwoman came. She ordered all of us who recovered from illness to get in formation. Thinking that we were going to be dispatched to work all the ill attempted to get up. But she immediately ascertained the deception.[118]

Very few of us remain. The watchwoman selected eight of us, and which included me, and announced that we will be the "funeral corps." Up to this time there was a massive clutter as the dead would lay in the barracks for several days. Now we had the responsibility to immediately undress and remove the gold teeth from the dead, and four of us to carry and place them at the barrack's door. Then the camp funeral command was supposed to drive by each morning and evening and haul away the corpses.

I do not know how I can carry another when I can barely move myself. My eyes go in circles, my feet collapse from under me. To walk I need to hold to the wall.

We approach one woman who died this morning. I take her cold foot but I cannot lift it, although the decease's body is totally emaciated. The other three women are lifting her but I am in no condition. The watchwoman slaps me in the face and

---

[118] Those who were ill knew they would be immediately sent to the crematorium if they would not rise.

shoves a pair of scissors and flat-nose pliers into my hands. I am supposed to undress them and remove the gold teeth. But if I should dare to appropriated even one then I will accompany my patients to my forefathers.

They place the dead woman at my feet. I look at her, she seems to be alive! Her eyes are opened and appear to be moving! But the watchwoman is hurrying me to undress her. I timidly poke her in the side – she is cold. So why the eyes? Finally I guess they are reflecting the lamp hanging from the ceiling and which the wind is swaying. With shaking hands I cut off her dress. I try to pick her up to remove the dress from under her but her body does not stay in one spot and slides back, knocking her head against the floor. So I need to hold her close to myself to do this. But her body is so cold. As though laughing at me the deceased woman flashes her gold teeth in the light. What am I to do? No way can I pull them out! I look around if the watchwoman is watching, quickly I close her mouth with the pliers. Will the watchwoman check?

But the watchwoman nevertheless noticed. She hits me so hard that I fall over the corpse. I jump up. And she was waiting just for this. She begins to beat on me with this heavy stick and aiming right at my head. It seems that my head has burst in half while the watchwoman does not stop. There is blood on the floor.

She kept beating me until she had to catch her breath.

The entire passageway is loaded with corpses. They need to be undressed. But I cannot. No way can I do this. It would be better for me to carry them, slide them using the last of my strength, but not to undress them! Maybe someone will be sorry for me, but I cannot. I am sick, so sick.

Another started to undress them.

Walking away the watchwoman opened the washroom for us. She said we could wash and spend the night here. But sadly enough there is no water. It is only called a washroom.

The concrete floor is cold, but at least it does not stick so bad. The women lie down. I would also lie, but my beaten head hurts so much that I cannot lay it down. I supported my forehead with my fingers and sat.

I nonetheless somehow fell asleep, because when I awoke I was shivering from the cold. It appears we were sopping wet. Icy water was dripping straight down on us from the pipes that served as a shower.

We ran into the barrack. We informed everyone that water was running, they all awoke and rushed to the washroom. But the water, as if cursed, stopped running. Some women drank from the puddles that formed on the floor, but for others this was still not enough.

In our block of barracks, 40 to 60 women died each day. At our door there is constantly piled a mount of petrified blue corpses. The wagon arrives and with a team of inmates. Two men take the gaunt and frozen corpse, one by the hands, the other by the feet, swing it and throw it to the top of the pile of the same kind of naked corpses.

The crematorium operates around the clock every day and large mounts of corpses are piled near it. About a thousand persons die each day at the camp.

The inmates who bury the remains arrived with good news: the front is getting closer!

The men are being evacuated. We saw how three groups were led away. There are also less SS agents. It is obvious the camp is being liquidated. Those capable of working leave first, while they will probably cremate us with the barracks.

The women will also be evacuated.[119]

A supervisor arrived early in the morning and announced that those who are in a condition to walk on their own must be ready to leave at any time. I am not able to walk on my own.

[119] Evacuation of Stutthof camp begin January 25, 1945.

Here is the end. And just when freedom is so close I am giving up my last breath. If I only had a little bit more strength. Just a drop of hope and I will survive!

Just before evening this same German officer again came and ordered us into formation. All who possibly could left the barrack. I looked around. All that remained in the barrack were corpses and those who had no strength to even sit. No, I will not stay! Not for any reason will I stay! I will go! If something should happen to me, at least it will not be here! Anything, but not to just lie here and wait until they cremate me.

Rocking sideways I exit. Only one relatively healthy woman remains in the barrack: she does not want to abandon her dying friend at her final moment.

They lead us away. What a large mass we were when we initially arrived and what a pitiful handful is departing. And even then not toward our freedom.

We spend the night at the same barrack that had no windows, we were here once already and just shivered in the cold.

In the morning we received a ration of bread: one-third of a quarter of a loaf of bread. We were warned that this is to suffice for three days. I guess this meant that the trip would take this long. But walking the entire time? I hope I can endure it!

Initially after I strolled awhile, I wanted to believe that I could walk the entire distance, but soon my legs started to bend under me. It seemed that I could not take even one more step. But nonetheless I forced my feet to take the next step, then one more, and again a few more. I would convince myself that soon they would allow us some rest. It was absolutely necessary for me to maintain myself until rest! Then it would be easier.

I almost completely fell by the time the convoy guard whistled and ordered us to sit on both sides of the road, along a ditch. I collapsed, closed my eyes, but the dirty snow along the road still gleamed in front of my eyes. This hardly refreshed my spirit. But neither the snow nor the icicles that I sucked the entire time helped me any.

It was hard to get up. But women helped me. I could not imagine that I would survive until evening.

When dusk was noticeable we were herded into some manor. Some were locked in the barn, others were herded into a shed. What a fortunate occasion, to lie the entire night to the very morning! I broke off a piece of bread and while chewing it started to cry: what a good decision it was not to remain at the camp. For sure by now, I would not be any more. But here I am so far still alive.

Two more days remain.

In vain did we hope that we would be on the road three days. The days passed but the end of the road was not in view. We walk and walk. No doubt they will herd us until the last of us collapses. Many women collapse along the road every day. They fall and are unable to get up even with the help of others. The convoy guards shoot one after another in the head, kick the body with their foot and the body rolls into a ditch. As they walk through the next village the convoy guards inform them that at so many kilometers from here is a corpse that must be buried. Soon it will get warm and an epidemic may begin.

Today a company of Soviet prisoners-of-war walked by us. They appear horrible: starved, yellow, emaciated. They look at us with the same empathy.

I strived not to miss any face, maybe my papa is among them?

I am being supported. I cannot walk on my own. Using the last of my strength I strive not to collapse on the women who are supporting me, I am doing my best to put my feet ahead of me one after another. But this is unbelievably difficult. In addition to all else my stride is more difficult due to the snow clinging to the wooden soles of my boots.

We are horribly starving: they give us nothing to eat. Sometimes one of the owners, at whose barn we are sheltered for the night, will give us a pail of potatoes. We each get one large or two small and we swallow the potatoes here in the shed. But this is so little.

We learned to recognize the snow-covered storage sheds, where potatoes or beets are stored for the winter. Not the hits, not even the shots of the convoy guards, were able to stop some of the staving women from scattering into a field, scraping away the snow with their stiff hands, digging into the ground and pulling out a beet. As we continue walking several dead are left behind in the trampled snow, their frozen hands still clenching the so-desired beet.

Some do return from a barn and bring to us, those too weak to go with them, a beet or potato. Unfortunately the storage sheds are often at a distance most of the days. To ameliorate my hunger I suck on snow and icicles.

I am starting to swell. The side on which I lie at night (there is not enough room to lie on your back), is swollen and causing my eyes to bulge, not until noon can I open them. It is horrifying to look at my legs: they are so swollen and can barely fit into my large men's boots, those that earlier I had to stuff full of paper to fill the empty space. I am afraid that some morning I will not be able to shove them into the boots at all. But I cannot walk in the snow bare-footed. And I cannot risk what will happen if I do not remove them, it will be like the women whom we had to earlier wash [who did not remove theirs].

The further we travel the meaner the convoy guards get. It is obvious they are fed up with having to drag us, but they do not get tired as we do: every so many hours they are exchanged, they sit in a wagon that follows behind us with all their belongings and they rest there. We are only allowed to rest once each day, for a half-hour halt.

Occasionally at night deafening explosions are heard in the distance. Obviously the front. But during the day they again herd us further and the explosions are almost not heard. But to remain here is foolish. You will not hide in an empty barn, and if you decide to just lie still, this means you are too weak to travel and they will put a bullet into your head.

We are not the only ones dragging along this highway. An immensely long chain of wagons is stretched along it. Local Germans are hurrying to the west, further from the front, with their belongings and family piled on a wagon and their cows and sheep tied to it. It is strange that we who are awaiting the arrival of the front must move in the same direction with them. But we cannot turn to travel in the opposite direction: there are many convoys, they are armed, their dogs are vicious, while we are swollen, barely alive, unarmed.

We are already an entire week in Strellentin.[120] This was a former manor. The owner is in the military, the mistress and children fled to Berlin, and anything of value was pillaged by the neighbors.

They are holding us locked in the barns, while the *unterscharführer* with the guard is residing in the palace, now empty, deserted and desolate, a lone white structure on a hill.

They almost give us nothing to eat, only half a liter of what they call soup: dirty water without salt.

They only allow us out of the barns twice a day. So not to stiffen worse we must occupy ourselves with sports. In the mornings and evenings the watchwomen compel us to do exercises, while they roll over with laughter at this "sport event of the skeletons," as they nickname our pitiful attempts to imitate their movements. They arbitrarily selected some woman and brought her in front of the company and ordered

---

[120] Today known as Strzelecino, Poland, 40 miles northwest of Gdansk.

her to do the exercises solo, and then they compelled us to laugh at her. If someone did not laugh enough she got a hit on the head.

I am barely able to stand on my feel. For the "sports" other women pick me up and bring me. The watchwomen must not know that I am already in this condition.

Sadly, I am not the only one.

Explosions shook the ground the entire second half of today.

When it became dark the convoy guards unexpectedly ordered us to assemble. "We will go further." At night? This means – to be shot.

So we have not escaped death.

I will not go! I will remain. So the German soldiers do not notice I will seclude myself in a corner until I hear my fellow inmates walking away. And if they notice... Well, what is the difference, it will still be death, but just an hour sooner.

The women are trying to convince me to go. Maybe they are not taking us to be shot, maybe to travel further. But this will not save me anyway, I will not get far.

Nonetheless they drug me out of there. They did not want to leave such a young person to an obvious death. It was not noticeable in the darkness that they were dragging me, and maybe somehow I will manage.

We were ordered to walk very quietly. Even the convoy guards were prohibited to speak or smoke. They held the dogs by their collars and made sure they would not bark. Why such secrecy?

The silence is scary. The explosions that seemed close are not heard. A lot of snow is again stuck to my boots. My feet are not obeying me, I keep tripping. I have already fallen several times, but the women pick me up and drag me further. Do they not understand that this will be of no avail, that I am already helpless and even with their assistance I am in no condition to move? I am not even breathing, I just open my mouth and gasp for air. It is also apparent to them that now it is somewhat more difficult to drag me. They need to change places more often now. They beg me to hold on to them, not to slide out of their arms. But I fall. There is nothing more I can do.

The end.

I lie there. They lift me, but my legs no longer obey me, I cannot in any way overcome my weakness. The women are forced to let go of my arms, they are herded forward.

They walk away... Everyone is walking past me.

I close my eyes so not to watch how the convoy guard will shoot me.

I guess I am alive, only my side hurts. Maybe they just wounded me? I did not hear a gunshot and I did not feel pain. But why am I lying in a roadside ditch? The road is empty, this means, all have left. Yes, I can hearing the departing footsteps. So what happened here? Maybe he missed? Maybe. I have no wounds. But maybe he did not shoot? I did not hear anything. Of course! How did I not immediately guess that the convoy guard just pushed me into this ditch to get rid of me?

How pretty it is here! The silent forest, motionless. And much snow. Soft... Nice ... Quiet...

Whose voice is that? Am I having a hallucination? No, she is whispering. A woman's voice. She is asking if I am alive. But it is difficult to move my tongue.

The voice again asks if I am alive. I open one eye. Above me, on the highway, stands a woman. She orders me to climb out. I cannot lie there, otherwise I will freeze. I need to move.

But if I do not even have the strength to move, and not the ability to even talk?

She leaves me. At least I will be calm.

No, she returns. She brought a stick. What does she want?

For me not to fall asleep.

But I really need to sleep.

She tells me not to be stupid. Especially now when liberation is so close. I need to use my final strength to endure a while longer.

But I do not have any remaining final strength.

Nevertheless I need to endure. She will not leave me until I crawl out of this ditch. Even if on all fours, even if it takes until morning for me to pull myself from there, but I need to get out of here somehow. She will help. She will bring another stick.

Behind the forest again explosions can be heard. Maybe our own are indeed nearby? Somehow, one way or another, I need to get up.

My female deliverer laid on her stomach and pulled me by the hand. I slide forward and fall back again, and then try again to move forward. Exerting the last of my effort I somehow managed to crawl most of the way out. But to stand is very difficult. While I laid there it seems I gathered some strength, but in reality my weakness did not go away. My legs will not hold me up. My new friend gave me a stick and pulled me further. She ordered me to clasp her hand and at least move a little bit, so not to freeze.

I am leaning on this stick as she pulls me by the hands.

We are alone on this long empty highway. On both sides of us is forest. But it seems that someone is staring at us from behind each tree, watching us.

It is also scary for my companion, obviously, as she does not stop talking. She is from Hungary, a school teacher. Her entire family was shot, beginning with her parents, then husband. He was a good person and her parents were good people. Now she remains alone, completely orphaned. She cannot imagine how she will live, but she does not want to die. This is why she gave this facial expression that she was exhausted: she decided to stay back and wait for the Red Army. She heard how one convoy officer gave another the *unterscharführer's* directive: not to shoot, even if someone should collapse, as the sound will give their location away.

Suddenly, "*Hände hoch!*"[121] We raise our shaking hands. Out from the forest runs an armed German soldier with a dog. He orders us to give up our weapons. He does not believe we do not have any, he searches us. He demands our documents. We reply we have none because we are from the concentration camp, we are inmates that were recently driven along this road. It became difficult for us and we fell behind, but now we feel better and so are trying to catch up to them.

But the German soldier does not want to hear our story. He confirms that we are Russian spies, and he needs to shoot us. We assure him that we are from the camp. Would spies walk in public dressed as we are? But he has his opinion: we are traitors and are waiting for the Russians to arrive.

Another German soldier appears from somewhere. It appears that he knows of our camp, and which definitely passed in this direction and as though stopped at the village Khin.

The first German soldiers brings out from behind a tree a bicycle he hid there, sits on it and orders us to follow behind. He warns us that we should not attempt to run, since he will then release his dog which will swallow us in just a few mouthfuls.

He pedals and we do our best not to fall behind. I cannot seem to breathe, I fall... But after hearing the mean barks of the dog I force myself to move. My friend supports me.

Finally we reach this small house. The German soldier orders the dog to guard us and then enters the house. The dog does not move his eyes from us. He just waits for us to make a move. The cursed animal has his eyes on my neck. I am sure he has gnawed more than just one person to death.

---

[121] Meaning, "Hands up!"

Now it is bright daylight. Unexpectedly we saw a convoy guard from our camp approaching in a jeep. He beats us up and orders us to climb into the cart. I barely make it.

They take up through some village. It is desolate. Not one living soul. The shutters are closed, doors are locked. Silence. But maybe the people are still sleeping?

Beyond the village are fields. In the distance near an immense barn are many jeeps. Apparently this will be our next camp. All is beginning all over again.[122]

A horrible sound. One after another we hear deafening explosions. The guard's dog sitting next to us became alerted. The German soldiers we see at the barns seem to be killing time. Some look at the sky, others argue among themselves.

We drive up. What is going on? The guards are rolling barrels to the barns! They are going to burn the place down. We will be cremated alive!

They push us into the barns. There are many women there, and not just from our camp. Lying on ground mixed with bran, straw and manure are dead and dying persons. To them all is already lost.

Should I tell them or not? I will be silent. Better for them not to know, they will be calmer.

No, I will tell them. At least one.

I whisper this horrible news to the neighbor on my left. But apparently she did not understand me, or did not hear, explosions echo around us. I tell another. She screams and rushes to a crack in the wall to take a look. But nothing is seen through the crack. No German soldiers, no smoke. Fear overwhelms many others. All start to bang, stir. But no one sees anything. The guards are gone.

The air raid siren. They are coming! Airplanes? Someone outside.

---

[122] This was the village Lanz, in the state Brandenburg, Germany.

They shake my shoulder. "Who are you?" Then the Hungarian woman speaks. She asks if I understand Polish. What is he saying?[123]

He is shouting that the Red Army is already in the village, and the German soldiers have fled.

Maybe a provocation? No need to answer.

He is shouting, banging, but we are silent.

He repeats a second time and walks away.

It is quiet. But maybe the German soldiers did get scared by these explosions and fled, leaving us here alone?

Again the air raid siren. Something is approaching.

Why so much noise? Why are all crying? Where are they running? They will trample me! Help me stand, do not leave me alone!

No one is paying any attention to me. Women are running, hollering something as they hold their heads or stretch their hands forward. Tripping over dead bodies they fall, but they stand and run from the barn. But I cannot stand.

The girl next to me does not stand. She is dead. I will die right now if they do not pick me up.

I can hear male voices from outside the barn. Are they Red Army soldiers? Is it really them? I want out of here! Get me to them! How can I stand?

Red Army soldiers run into the barn. They hurry to us, they look for those alive and help them stand.

"Can I help you, little sister?"

They pick me up, put me on my feet, but I cannot move, my feet shake. Two Red Army soldiers clench their hands together like a chair and have me sit inside. Once comfortable they carry me out.

Ambulances are rushing to the barn from the village, more Red Army soldiers are arriving. One offered to help carry me to it, another gave me some bread, a third gave me his gloves. I

---

[123] A man outside is trying to communicate to the inmates in the barn.

am so glad for their goodness that tears flowed on their own. The soldiers are comforting and calming us, while one pulled out his handkerchief and wiped my tears.

"Do not cry, little sister, we will not let them hurt you ever again."

And on his hat shined a red star. It has been so long since I saw one![124]

---

[124] The liberation occurred here on March 10, 1945. Rolnikaite was under German occupation 3 years, 7 months and 15 days. The travel from Stutthof to Lanz was about 45 days, a distance of about 300 miles.

APPENDIX

INTERVIEW OF MARIA ROLNIKAITE

BY TATYANA VOLTSKAYA

February 5, 2003

(Translated from the Russian)

Tatyana Voltskaya:

Maria Rolnikaite is a writer and a former inmate of Nazi camps. Maria Rolnikaite was forced to experience what is located beyond the limit of literature. As a teenager she was confined in the Vilnius ghetto, from the ghetto she was transferred to a concentration camp, and then to an extermination camp. Her father remained alive, and also served on the front. Her mother and younger brother and sister perished. Maria Rolnikaite's book, *I Must Tell*, is dedicated to their memory. Notes served as its basis; she took these with fanatical intensity, at the risk of her life at the beginning of the German occupation. She is like Anna Frank. But Anna Frank perished, leaving us only a documented witness of the tragedy that received the appellation of holocaust. But Maria Rolnikaite and only by a miracle lived through it and survived, and she can herself explain her fate and the fate of her book.

Maria Rolnikaite:

I was born in Klaipeda, in Lithuania, into a family of attorneys. There I attended Lithuanian school, although at home we spoke Yiddish. Papa always influenced us, that we live in a small city, and we should not adapt and become like the others of the province. He dreamed of sending me and my sister to study in Paris. Although this was beyond his means, grandmother promised to help, and we had an uncle who lived in Paris. He was an attorney also and said we would live in some kind of dormitory, and he would help us and take us in on our days off.

Tatyana Voltskaya:

Several years would go by when Maria's uncle would heroically perish at some concentration camp. Knowing French he would often intervene on behalf of his friends to the camp authorities. He was one of the organizers of the university in fetters. He was taken at night to be shot, in a truck together with his coffin. They say that an SS agent kicked his dead body with his foot and said the words, "He was a real man."

Maria Rolnikaite:

When Lithuania became Soviet, there was no more discussion about Paris. The Germans surfaced in Vilnius within two days after the beginning of the war. Attempting to evacuate, papa separated from us on the first day. We then found out that he voluntarily entered the army, while we – mama, my older sister and two youngsters, 5 and 7 years of age – returned home. And we shook hoping the guard would not turn us in. Because if we were to just mention that someone wanted to join the Bolsheviks, then they would categorically execute him.

Tatyana Voltskaya:
On September 6, 1941, the family was locked in the ghetto.

Maria Rolnikaite:
These were several narrow streets in the center of the city, barricaded by a high, brick prison-style wall. A poor district. In essence the area where poor Jews lived. A few Lithuanians and Poles where there, but they were relocated. They were herded and shot, and we moved into their homes. There were 18 persons living in one apartment. Not enough room for all of us. One girl slept on the table, another under the table, one in the tub; not in the bathroom, but right in the tub. And one family took up the entire kitchen.

Tatyana Voltskaya:
To keep a diary was in fashion among the Lithuanian students at the time. It was filled with notes about grades, books and personal secrets. Maria Rolnikaite also loved to write verses and stories about beautiful princesses. But with the beginning of the war she started to record what was occurring around her.

Maria Rolnikaite:
When the Germans arrived, immediately, on the second or on the third say, there appeared announcements on the streets, that Jews are obligated to wear these yellow stars. Initially it was the letter *J* – standing for Jew, then that Jews cannot walk on the sidewalk, cannot be in public alone, cannot enter stores or cafes. Even taxis were required to hang a sign that Jews were not allowed. And it was embarrassing for me to go into the street with this yellow mark. What if I suddenly encounter a friend or teacher? So I continued to sit home and write my diary. This became a habit. So I wrote all of what was occurring here. And then I as if saw a map of the world. It was the one

that hung in class at school. And I understood that Hitler was not everywhere, that war was not everywhere. And people will continue to live there after the war. So let them know the truth.

Tatyana Voltskaya:
Then Maria Rolnikaite heard many positive statements regarding her conduct at the time, but she could not accept them.

Maria Rolnikaite:
This was my infantile stubbornness. The war started, I was a month short of 14 years of age. And this is how I prolonged my project. There was a problem with paper in the ghetto. But nevertheless since there were many old apartments it was possible to find old notebooks. Once someone gifted me a accounting ledger where all the pages were almost clean. And right now I am amazed: no one dared to laugh at such a homebred chronicler. On the contrary, they would tell me, "Masha, did you write about this? Did you record something about this?" Four of us slept there, on the floor of course and near the window, and half of the window sill, was our territory. That is where all of my notes lay.

Tatyana Voltskaya:
But half of the window sill did not seem a reliable place for notes.

Maria Rolnikaite:
Our principal executioner, Franz Murer, imposed these *aktions* (as these roundups for execution were called). So in autumn 1941, they were massive, 3 to 5 thousand at a time. And then when only an indispensable quantity of artisans remained, and which were so necessary for them to have, he could not kill any more of them. Then he invaded some arbitrary apartment and

implemented a search. If there was a piece of clothing without this yellow star, if there was a piece of bread not from the batch distributed (since they baked it for us, although it was more like clay), he said we were conducting a business. Then he would take the residents into custody: those in one apartment one time, a 100 next time, 300 another time, as many as entered his mind. And so this danger always hung over my notes. He would haul everyone to be shot, not only us, but including the neighbors. And although we were always short on matches, on top of all of my notebooks was a box with two matches. I would feel so bad if I had to do this, but mama said for me to memorize it all. So if I survive so will all of these notes.

Tatyana Voltskaya:
Maria learned from her experiences. She hauled buckets of water for an immense garden. Over 100 buckets a day. And this helped. In the book, *I Must Tell.*

Announcer
"There was a pogrom in Shnipeshk. Villains started a bonfire and forced the Rabbi and some bearded elders to attend. They ordered them to throw the Torah into the fire with their own hands, and which they stole from the synagogue. They forced the elders to undress and they took them by the hands and forced them to dance around the bonfire and sing *Katusha*. Then they would scorch them with the fire and pull out their beards, beat them up and again force them to dance. Was this really true? It is really possible to ridicule people this way?"[125]

Maria Rolnikaite:
When the ghetto was liquidated, within two years, we found out they were taking us to be shot. But apparently at one camp,

---

[125] Quoted from *I Must Tell.*

this one in Shtraznov,[126] workers were needed. We were ordered to walk in front of soldiers one by one. My sister, before this time, succeeded in escaping from the ghetto and she survived. I walked out and a soldier grabbed me by the coat, "Go over there." I look and a series of soldiers are standing across the street. There behind them people are standing and among them my mother with the children. Then it came to my mind that those standing there were either the aged or with children. I ran to this soldier and said, "Please let me go. My mother is over there. We are one family." It was obvious to mama that only young people were on my side of the street. She hollered, "Do not come here. You are young, you need to work. Live, even if you alone survive." And she picked up sister Rayechka in her hands, then brother Ruvik and he waved to me with his hand. I never saw them after this.

Tatyana Voltskaya:
Maria's hardships started here. The young people were forced into a railway boxcar and sent away. Standing of course. And not knowing where of course. All thought to Ponary, to the forest to be shot.

Maria Rolnikaite:
It appeared they brought us at night to this forest. These were barracks. And I did not know what these people were doing at night in their pajamas and why they were jumping out of windows.

Tatyana Voltskaya:
The pajamas were actually inmates uniforms. And jumping out of the windows was one form of concentration camp punishments.

---

[126] Referring to Strasdenhof.

Maria Rolnikaite:

These were men from the Riga ghetto. In general this camp was called Kaiserwald. This horrible watchwoman was there, she was always hitting us on the head with her lash. We were ordered to leave our belongings behind and they herded us into this barrack. On the next day 50 persons at a time were herded into another barrack where the sign read, "Bathhouse." But we knew that they called the crematorium a bathhouse. This is why we knew we on our way to a certain death. We arrived. They ordered us to undress. With German meticulousness we had to place our coat, dress and underclothes in separate piles. They only allowed us to wear our shoes. While in the boxcar I stood next to this one woman named Masha Mekhanik, she was a former teacher. Can you imagine the state I was in? I was just separated from my mother and the children. I told her all of this and told her about all of my notes. She was the first one to set me straight, "Masha, save your notes."[127] She started to grab them out of my hands, crumple them and shove them into her boots. And so did another woman. Bewildered I also did the same. And were shoving and I was shoving. At this moment the German woman walked up to me and suddenly hit me on the head with her lash. But I was still able to crumple and shove several pages into one boot.

Tatyana Voltskaya:

Soon after the woman whose name was Masha Mekhanik was no longer.

Maria Rolnikaite:

Because several men escaped she was taken into custody. We were arranged into formation and they selected every third person. Since a person was prohibited from turning their head,

---

[127] Both of them are named Masha

I looked sideways and said, "Masha, I am ninth." But she said, "No, I am."

Tatyana Voltskaya:
Once settled in the barrack the women returned the girl her notes. Knowing them from memory she was able to restore what was lost. It is true that there were no pencils or paper in the camp?

Maria Rolnikaite:
We worked at a construction site, and empty bags of cement were laying all over the place. We wrapped our feet in them, because they did not give us stockings.

Tatyana Voltskaya:
So you were able to use these paper sacks for something that was prohibited.

Maria Rolnikaite:
Masha advised me to start a buzz that I need pencils. And although the punishment for conversation was 25 hits with a stick, we were nevertheless successful while pushing wheeled carts full of rocks.

Tatyana Voltskaya:
Maria Rolnikaite seems to find within herself the strength to joke, that she has a special vocation: hauling wheeled carts full of rocks. And then they assigned her to break rocks. Fragments flew into her face. Up to this time she does not know how she survived. Someone threw her a pencil stub. She restored her diary and continued to write. To hide them was an art of its own.

Maria Rolnikaite:
When we would find out that there will be a search, we took them into another barrack. Or we would hide them behind the discharge pipes in the toilet in our barrack. Then they transferred us out of Shtraznov, and we were less of a quantity, and took us to Stutthof. Riga was now under attack. We could hear the gunfire, we heard the bomb explosions.

Tatyana Voltskaya:
At this moment one more *aktion* was implemented: shooting everyone over the age of 30 and under the age of 18. Maria Rolnikaite still does not know to this time what miracle allowed three 17-year old girls to survive

Maria Rolnikaite:
At Stutthof my number was 60821. It was even more frightening as a crematorium was already there. Initially they took us to work at the Bauer estate, which was a manor. It was difficult, but we managed, although we slept in the pigs' pen. But when we gathered the harvest we would grab and eat the green kernels as we fed the pigs, or some small potatoes. Then they told us, "We will only give you the amount you are supposed to get." This was one loaf of bread for the entire week. And he threatened us, "If you will work poorly, or just pretend or get ill, then I will send you straight into the crematorium." He liked to vex us this way. It was difficult there, but this one French prisoner-of-war worked there. Somehow I started a French tune to get his attention, and then I somehow related to him not to work so fast. When I was ordered to take four horses and harness them to a wagon and drive some hay – and my height only reached to the horse's belly – this Frenchman took me and saddled me. I did not know how to milk cows. Initially when I tried milking all of it ran down my arms. Behind me stood the mistress, the boss' sister, a near-sighted old spinster,

she kicked me so hard in my back that I was thrown against the cow's stomach, and then I quickly learned to milk. My fingers figured what to do.

Tatyana Voltskaya:
In November, at the conclusion of work at the farm, we were back at the camp. They almost did not feed you there. The Red Army was close. All were begging to go to work, knowing that remaining in the camp meant certain death

Maria Rolnikaite:
Once they took us, and we thought it was to work. But they herded us into the bathhouse. Women were there lying on the floor with frostbitten hands and feet. It appears they also volunteered for work, they were taken to dig ditches, they stood in water up to their waist. How they wailed is indescribable and inexpressible. The German watchwoman gave me a pair of scissors to cut her boots off. I started to fumble. She hit me so hard and then pulled them off with pieces of meat from her feet. She screamed. What was principal was that these women would plead, "We will get well, we can work some more." But we were supposed to undress them and take them to the shower. We were ourselves on all fours or plainly just dragged them along the concrete floor. It was so horrifying, and no experience could be worse horrifying. And we understood that to volunteer for work was also not a deliverance.

Tatyana Voltskaya:
Did these women perish?

Maria Rolnikaite:
Of course. They were taken to the crematorium. Then on the eve of the year 1945, the fuel storage shed burned down. We felt this was an act of sabotage. Of course, they never put

anyone in the oven for cremation alive, they had to first die. They dug this pit and the pit is still there today.

In 1987, I traveled to Stutthof, this was not the most rational decision that I made, but something drew me there. I went into the actual crematorium. There were three ovens. I wondered in which one of them they were going to shove me? And so they dug these pits, lengthwise and across the tracks. They would place the deceased on the rails, push them into the oven, while a fire burned from under them. They were incinerated and the ashes fell into this pit. So what does this tell us?

Tatyana Voltskaya:
You were able to preserve your notes even if you had to tie them to your arms. Good that your clothing was wide and you had to raise your arms during a search while they felt your torso. No one ever expected to remain alive. And suddenly this order came for all of those capable of walking to evacuate into another camp.

Maria Rolnikaite:
I could not walk. I thought I would collapse. But I knew that whoever would not persevere would get a bullet in the back of the head, and this was better than being cremated alive in these barracks. And so I crawled out. I went. This road was called the road of death. First, what we wore, what they called boots, had wooden soles and glued along the top. The snow would stick to it. It was the end of February. It was difficult to walk and they held me up by my arms and carried me. It would be pitiful to leave behind such a young girl.

Tatyana Voltskaya:
It would have been sadder since everyone knew and loved Maria. But it is not surprising that at an extermination camp

there existed independence, in which Maria became a serious participant.

Maria Rolnikaite:
While there I wrote what I called the *Daily Express*, or some kind of a newspaper that was passed along person to person. In addition to this I composed the *Strasdenhof hymn*, that we are building a new Europe, only that the soup is very watery since we have no potatoes yet, while our shoes are walking here on their own. This was irony.

Tatyana Voltskaya:
How were you able to do this under such circumstances?

Maria Rolnikaite:
We moved two tables together in the barrack, this became our stage. I walked out and like a stupid schoolgirl I gave a curtsy, but it seemed that no one understood that this was a curtsy. Initially I was very agitated, and when I noticed that people were smiling at me, then the inside of me calmed. One girl played a tune on her comb. We sang *Evening Bells*, and everyone cried. Some read some poetry. One person remembered a classic passage and recited by memory. As far as songs were concerned there was my *Strasdenhof hymn*, and then another similar song I named *Sport*. It had to do with getting a sport-compote if the person was late for roll-call.

The sport consisted of jumping like a frog. This was very horrible. For the next several days I was hardly able to breathe. But this Hans ran between the rows and watched to make sure we were not pretending, but were actually jumping.

Tatyana Voltskaya:
Maybe due to remembering the independent presentation of Maria Rolnikaite in the barracks the women drug her with

their final strengths through the snow even though not knowing where. In the book, *I Must Tell*.

Announcer:
"We learned to recognize the snow-covered storage sheds, where potatoes or beets are stored for the winter. Not the hits, not even the shots of the convoy guards, were able to stop the staving women from scattering into a field, scraping away the snow with their stiff hands, digging into the ground and pulling out a beet. When we leave several dead are left behind in the trampled snow, their frozen hands still clenching the so-desired beet."[128]

Maria Rolnikaite:
For the most part we were herded during the day, while at night they would shove us into some shed or some building at an estate. If it was a good one, they would boil us some potatoes and each would get 1 or 2 spoonfuls. If not, then nothing. My legs swelled to such a size that my legs were the same width as my waistline. I was afraid not to remove my shoes. I would groan so bad when I removed them in the evening, but the groans were worse in the morning when I had to shove my swollen feet into them. The final few days they did not move us anywhere and suddenly late at night, and it was pitch-black darkness, they ordered us to move. Later did we find out, after the liberation, they were moving us away from the Red Army, as they could already hear the explosions from the bombing. Along the road wagons belonging to local Germans were passing us up, filled with personal belongings with a cow or goat tied to it. They were also fleeing from the Russians and figured we were part of them. We still had the order to move on, but as we found out later this place was liberated by Katyusha rocket launchers, and their echo was heard in the forest, and so this disoriented the Germans, not knowing the

---

[128] Quoted from *I Must Tell*.

direction of the invasion. They explained to us that we were surrounded, and so what happened is that the Germans were leading us directly into encountering the Red Army. But I did not know this at the time and we walked and walked and then I finally collapsed. The women tried to lift me, but the Germans were prodding them to move, and I told them to just leave me behind, and they did.

Tatyana Voltskaya:
Maria fell into a roadside ditch with the sole desire to die by freezing. They did not shoot her, because there was a order not to shoot so not to get the attention of the Russians. One of her female friends exerted the effort and got her back on her feet.

Maria Rolnikaite:
We walked arm in arm. She was a teacher from Hungary. She said her entire family perished, but she wanted to live. And suddenly some German soldier jumped out from behind some trees. "Halt! You are spies." We tried to explain that we are not spies, but from a local camp and so wearing these striped clothes. Fortunately another soldier or officer surfaced and who knew that our camp did pass along this road, and he said, "Yes, yes, they were taken to the village Khin." This is how I know the village where we were liberated. They put us on a jeep with some trained dogs, and the dogs were trained to go for the throat. And they led us through the sleeping village.

On the other side of the village was an immense structure, either a shed or stable and they shoved us in there. We watched them bring some barrels of gasoline to it. And I said, "Better for me to have died where I was." But we decided not to say anything so no to cause a panic and make matters worse. But we had our noses open to smell smoke. And then we hear someone banging on the door and saying in Polish, "Hey, women, come out, the Red Army is in the village."

Tatyana Voltskaya:
Initially no one believed it, thinking that it was a provocation, wanting all of them to run out of it and so then shoot them in the backs. So no one, of the several hundred persons packed in it, moved from their spot.

Maria Rolnikaite:
He said, "Are all of you so stupid that you still sit there?" And he left. We started to think, maybe he is right? This seemed unbelievable that we would actually remain alive.

Tatyana Voltskaya:
The soldier told the Soviet tank drivers that prisoners were in the barn.

Maria Rolnikaite:
This soldier used one of the tanks to pull down the crossbeam on the front of the barn and then he hollered, "Long live freedom." And the women ran screaming, they were hysteric, hands ahead of them, shouting. But I was afraid that I would right now be trampled underfoot and so I just laid there. I said, "Take me also." No one heard me. They are all running. Red Army soldiers entered and walked toward me, they picked me up, I was still able to stand, but not able to walk. They wove their arms together and made me a seat into which I climbed. I hugged them both by the neck and they carried me into the village. This was the first time that I cried since I separated from my mother. I did not actually cry, tears just started to flow on their own. He said to me, one of the soldiers, "Don't weep, little sister, we will not allow you to be hurt anymore." And I had one thought on my mind, "They will not kill me."

Tatyana Voltskaya:
Reflections on the events, meeting father and your older sister, the complexity with documents, life without a passport, the

suspicion of those around you, finally, your entrance into the Literary Institute, as bitter all of this was, you hid the surviving and reconstructed notes.

Nevertheless the book is published and reprinted. Maria Rolnikaite paid her debt, the debt of the living on behalf of the dead. It would be a great relief if you could today say that the events of this book were not actual. But regretfully, it is not this way.

Maria Rolnikaite:
I have to admit that it is very actual.

I Must Tell

CPSIA information can be obtained
at www.ICGtesting.com
Printed in the USA
LVHW032001271221
707267LV00012B/1942